TRANSFORMED by LOVE

EMPOWERED to SERVE

Graeme & Julia Cann

Transformed by Love. Empowered to Serve © Copyright: Graeme & Julia Cann, 2026

All rights reserved. No part of this publication may be reproduced, stored in a retrieval system or transmitted in any form by any means, electronic, mechanical, photocopying, recording or otherwise, without the prior permission of the author — except in the case of brief quotation embodied in critical review and certain other non-commercial uses permitted by copyright law.

Cover design by Gary Lewis. Used with permission.

Transformed by Love. Empowered to Serve

1. Servanthood. 2. Christian Leadership. I. Title.

ISBN: 978-1-7641117-3-7

All scripture references (unless specified) from the New Living Translation (NLT) © 2004, 2007, 2013, 2015. Used with permission.

Table of Contents

Foreword		page V
Acknowledgements		page VII
Chapter 1	An Intriguing Journey	page 8
Chapter 2	A Prophetic Picture	page 16
Chapter 3	Servanthood in the Old Testament	page 26
Chapter 4	The Promised Servant	page 36
Chapter 5	Jesus: the Ultimate Servant	page 44
Chapter 6	Servanthood Empowered by the Spirit	page 54
Chapter 7	Formed by the Spirit to Serve	page 64
Chapter 8	Creating a Serving Community	page 74
Chapter 9	Serving in the Early Church	page 82
Chapter 10	Paul's Instructions to Timothy	page 90
Chapter 11	The Shepherd Model of Leadership	page 98
Chapter 12	Servanthood and Hierarchical Leadership	page 108
Chapter 13	Changed Lives. Empowered Leadership	page 120

FOREWORD

TRANSFORMED BY LOVE.
EMPOWERED TO SERVE.

What a challenging book from genuine servants of the Lord who have been living this perspective on leadership for many decades. In writing this book, Graeme and Julia Cann challenge us to deeply consider servanthood from a biblical perspective.

Selecting key passages of scripture, they interact with them highlighting practical application. The application is then reinforced with authentic personal stories and intentional principles for Church leaders. Furthermore, at the close of each of the well-paced chapters there is a helpful *'For Further Study'* section.

This is a masterful book — which when read and digested personally, could then be used for bible studies in Life Groups and within your Church leadership team.

I wholeheartedly recommend this book and pray that by God's grace, in applying the gems it contains, you and I too, may become genuine servant leaders.

Rev. Dr. Brian Birkett

Pastoral Church Consultant, Missionary and Author of *Healthy Pastors, Thriving Churches*

Acknowledgements

As we reflect on the creation of this book, we realise how indebted we are to so many people. Firstly, we are thankful to our family and friends for loving us, warts and all and setting us an example of love and acceptance that has greatly inspired and humbled us. We are grateful also to those who over the years have ministered to us and with us. Your acts of love and generosity to us and others have shaped us more than you can imagine.

We acknowledge those who have been directly involved in physically producing *Transformed By Love: Empowered To Serve*. We thank Dr. Brian Birkett for reading and critiquing the manuscript and for accepting our invitation to write the Foreword. Our thanks also go to Gary and Maree Lewis for proofreading the manuscript and to Gary for designing and preparing the book for publication. In addition we acknowledge the professionalism of Ingram Spark Australia in printing and promoting the book.

Finally, we acknowledge our heavenly Father to whom we owe everything that is precious to us. He is our source of life and light and understanding, and if this book is helpful to you we encourage you to give thanks to Him.

Graeme & Julia

Chapter One

An Intriguing Journey

CHAPTER ONE

Welcome to an Intriguing Journey.

"Then those righteous ones will reply, 'Lord when did we ever see you hungry and feed you? Or thirsty and give you something to drink? Or a stranger and showed you hospitality? Or naked and give you clothing? When did we ever see you sick or in prison and visit you?' And the King will say, 'I tell you the truth, when you did it to the least of these my brothers and sisters, you were doing it for me." (Matthew 25:37-40).

We were mesmerised as we watched her. She was a young Australian nurse working with The Leprosy Mission in Papua New Guinea. What captured our attention was that she was sitting on a stool with the foot of an old man in her lap and she was cleaning the most foul-smelling ulcer you can imagine. As she probed it for stones and thorns, she was quietly singing a hymn we knew well. "It is well with my soul." On her face was the most serene and peaceful expression and on the face of her patient, an unforgettable look of gratitude.

Serving God and others selflessly, with humility and dedication, is both a way of life and an expression of our gratitude to and love for our Heavenly Father. For

Christians, it has always been our highest act of worship.

This concept is deeply rooted in the teaching of the Bible, where the commitment to serve is presented as an alternative way of living, compared with being motivated by our own needs and desires. It involves seeking to know the mind of God and following the example set by Jesus, "who came not to 'be served, but to serve, and to give His life a ransom for many." (Mark 10:45). Biblical servanthood is characterized by acts of kindness and compassion and a willingness to help others, thereby reflecting the love and grace of God, given to us through Jesus Christ.

Let us offer some important definitions. Biblical servanthood is an attitude of the heart; 'a servant' is a designation. Jesus told His disciples, "I no longer call you servants. I call you friends." Biblical servanthood is the attitude of a grateful friend, not the attitude of a slave, and it always results in joyful and loving service. Mother Teresa once famously said, "Work without love is slavery."

Biblical servanthood is not 'servitude'. Servitude describes the occupation of a slave. We are not slaves of God. We are emancipated slaves, who are now children of God. As children of God, we freely offer ourselves completely to Him as our act of worship.

This act of worship involves engaging in the kind of serving that includes 'feeding the hungry, giving drink to the thirsty, giving hospitality to the stranger, clothing the naked and visiting the sick and those in prison and every other expression of mercy and compassion.

We are commanded to imitate Jesus, the ultimate

servant, and there are multiple reasons why the whole Church and the wider community should strive to understand the importance of Biblical servanthood.

When serving God and others, is the result of aligning our actions and attitudes with the teachings and example of Jesus Christ, we continue to develop a deeper connection with God, and as we do, our faith in Him and His promises, increases.

Serving God and others as the primary purpose of our lives cultivates virtues such as humility, compassion, kindness and selflessness. These qualities, taught consistently throughout the New Testament, are essential in every aspect of our life.

In our early marriage we served in the Leprosy Mission. It was at that time we became familiar with the inspiring story of Mary Verghese. Mary, who was born in India in 1922, became an Indian physician. She suffered spinal injuries in a car accident but despite that, she became a pioneer surgeon in the field of rehabilitation.

At the Christian Medical Centre at Vellore, under the tutelage of Dr Paul Brand, she pioneered life-changing surgery on the crippled hands of leprosy patients. Her life was rooted in her faith in Jesus Christ and her humility, kindness and selflessness was cultivated by her commitment to serving God.

In a world often characterised by self-centredness, individualism, discrimination, egotism, and materialism, the biblical principles of servanthood offer a countercultural alternative. They emphasise the importance of caring for others. It encourages us to look beyond our personal goals and needs and make a positive impact on the lives of those we live among.

Practising biblical servanthood improves relationships by fostering such qualities as empathy, understanding and respect. It encourages individuals to prioritise the needs of others, leading to stronger and more resilient connections with family, friends and colleagues. This is particularly important when it comes to marriage.

It is disturbing for us as we reflect on the many times we have heard Christians talking about the topic of ... *'husbands' headship' and 'wives' submission'* as if it were a division of power and servitude. For husbands — to be told that they are the 'head' and commanded to love their wives — their greatest act of 'love and headship' is to serve her selflessly. For wives — to be told to 'submit to' and to 'honour' their husbands — their greatest act of 'love and submission' is to serve him selflessly. It ends up being the same thing: a decision to not focus on our own needs and desires, but on the real needs and desires of our spouse. This is genuine servanthood being lived out practically and selflessly.

In every age, the most important question of what it means to live a meaningful life, calls each person in every generation to examine their values and motivations. For many people, personal fulfillment is sought in achievements or possessions, yet history and the wisdom of the Bible suggest a different and deeper path: one of humble service. The primary reason for writing this book is our growing conviction that the purpose of humanity is to serve God and each other, and the world's growing disregard for this truth lies at the root of all social dislocation, relational disconnection and national and international aggression.

We are also concerned that much of what passes as leadership in the Church, flies in the face of the teaching and example of Jesus Christ, and indeed, of all the teaching of both the Old and New Testaments on servanthood. The elevation and veneration of men and women who hold leadership positions in the Church, but are merely servants, called by God to serve Him and others, mimics the privilege and prestige we give to leaders in secular contexts and is, we believe, a major contributor to disunity, apathy and disaffection in the universal Church.

Do we believe that Spirit-filled leadership in the Church is an essential element? YES! When Jesus commissioned believers to build His Church, through evangelism and disciple making, it was clear that such a task would require leadership. The apostles were the original models. Fully convinced that Jesus was the Christ, the Son of God, and filled with the Holy Spirit, they committed themselves to sacrificial service, driven by a clear vision to mobilise and equip believers to fulfil Christ's commission. They made sacrifices and they made disciples as they had been instructed. They served others and equipped them to be servants like themselves. Each of their lives reflected the life of the Christ who had washed their feet.

Do we believe that servant leadership is an alternative leadership model to hierarchical leadership? NO! It is not a leadership model. Servant leadership is a way of life that God's children embrace as their highest act of gratitude and worship.

Do we believe that Jesus taught that true servants of God become the best leaders? YES! They become leaders transformed by love and empowered to serve.

FOR FURTHER STUDY

Read Mattew 25:31-46. Jesus particularly mentions caring for the hungry and thirsty, the homeless, the desperately poor, the sick and the prisoners. Who is it in your world that God is calling you to serve?

Read Mark 10:45. In what ways did Jesus' ministry demonstrate servanthood?

Read Philippians 2:1-12. Paul mentions three of the qualities of servanthood in this passage: humility, sacrifice and obedience. How would you describe the function of these qualities in the lives of the servants of God that you know?

Chapter Two

A Prophetic Picture

CHAPTER TWO

Adam and Eve — A Prophetic Picture

"Then God said, "Let us make humankind in our own image, in the likeness of ourselves and let them rule over the fish in the sea, the birds in the air, the animals, and over all the earth and over every crawling creature that crawls on the earth.

So, God created humankind in his own image; in the image of God, he created him: male and female he created them. God blessed them: God said to them, 'Be fruitful and multiply, fill the earth and subdue it. Rule over the fish in the sea, the birds in the air and every living creature that crawls on the earth." Then God said, "Here! Throughout the whole earth I am giving you as food, every seed-bearing plant and every tree with seed bearing fruit."

Genesis 1:26-29 (TCJB))

This passage is summed up with the words, *"God saw everything He had made, and indeed it was very good."* God was delighted with what he had made.

Delighted! Ecstatic! Joyful!

The harmony of creation and its ability to care for and reproduce itself, delighted Him. He was ecstatic about the creation of the man and the woman, made in His image and capable of entering the deepest of all intimacies with Him and with each other. Whilst He was the Creator and sustainer of all that He had made, He invited the man and the woman to share in the wonder of it all. Adam, by naming the animals and both by cultivating and caring for the garden of Eden.

It is clear, from the outset that the man and woman were not just being invited to enjoy this amazing connectedness with God, but to serve Him and the world He had created for them. As cultivators and carers, they were servants of the Creator not out of obligation — but as their very highest act of gratitude and worship.

This beautiful image can be seen as a prophetic statement with deep significance for both Israel and the Church. It proclaims that God's perfect will is for humanity's relationship with Him to be completely restored. Not only were we created, but now we are redeemed, and like Adam and Eve, we are meant to live in unbroken fellowship with Him and with each other. Our service and our worship of Him should be an expression of our gratitude and obedience.

In pondering the truth in Ephesians 2:10 that we "*are Gods workmanship, created in Christ Jesus to do good works, which God prepared in advance, for us to do...*" we decided to focus on the word 'work', converting it into an acrostic.

Willingness

   Obedience.

      Renewal and **R**estoration.

      Kingdom ministry.

Let's take a deeper look at each of them.

WILLINGNESS: Biblical servanthood begins with a Holy Spirit driven desire to see the Father's will being fulfilled in us. From the very beginning, God invited Adam and Eve into a working relationship with Himself. It was to be a relationship born out of worship and awe that saw them sustaining and caring for His creation. Their practical involvement began with His invitation and depended on their willingness to co-operate with His purposes.

So it is with us today. God has called His children to work with Him, and His purposes are clear. He has come to redeem the world through sacrificial love, and He invites us to love one another and forgive one another as He has loved and forgiven us. Our willingness to co-operate with His purposes leads to sacrificial service. And our example is Jesus, who said in John 9:5, *"We must carry out the works assigned to us by the one who sent us. The night is coming and then no one can work. But while I am here in the world, I am the light of the world."* Jesus also said of us *"You are the light of the world"*.

Our friend Colin, is an outstanding example of one whose willingness to serve the Lord led to sacrificial, lifelong service to others. Born deaf, Colin bravely embraced what others saw as a disability, but what he saw was simply a hurdle to jump. As a young man he joined us at the Elkanah Christian Community. As a team member he was invaluable and inexhaustible. There was no job too lowly for him to do and no person too broken to befriend.

When we needed a Chapel, he went into the bush, found suitable logs and built a beautiful log Chapel single-handedly. When he needed a house, he did the same. But it was not just a house, it served as a retreat, where many a youth Group went to, over the years for teaching and encouragement. When it burnt down in the Black Summer fires, he built another house where he still provides hospitality for Church Youth Groups. His willingness to be *willing* to seek and follow God's purpose in his life, has resulted in great contentment for him and great blessing for others.

OBEDIENCE: Just as God's invitation to Adam and Eve was accompanied by a command they were expected to obey, God has given us one clear command. *"Love the Lord your God with all your heart, with all your soul and all your mind. This is the first and greatest commandment. A second is equally important; Love your neighbour as you love yourself."* (Matthew 22:37-39).

We are to love Him and love our neighbours. We are to live ordered lives, trusting Him whatever our circumstances. There are few religions in the world that claim they have only one old and one new command to obey and that they both are about love. Loving God and loving others.

Another valued colleague of ours was an elderly woman, May, who before coming to join the community lived alone. She loved on every hurting and broken person who came for help and support. She spoke words of encouragement to them and prayed with and for them. The gift she carried in her life was compassion and in obedience to God, she served Him and others lovingly.

***R**EFRESHED, RESTORED, RENEWED:* As rest was an important part of God's work-life balance, so too it must be with us. Sacrificial servanthood will always mean that we will need to be regularly renewed. If our task is to reflect God's love to others, we will need to actively receive that love, day by day and give ourselves the space to embrace it.

Service to others can sometimes leave us weary. All those who serve need regular times of refreshment. I (Julia) recall one of our most difficult times when, as a couple, Graeme suffered serious burnout. During the long recovery period, we rediscovered a principle that in our busyness we had forgotten. This was the principle of the Sabbath. Whilst for many people Sunday was their Sabbath, weekends were our busiest time of the week. With encouragement from others, we made Friday our day of rest and recreation. For us it became a day when our awareness of God's love for us was renewed.

***K**INGDOM WORK:* The final word in our acrostic is Kingdom work. Individuals, churches and missions all over the world are engaged in building God's Kingdom through sacrificial service.

Let us share a moving story of a Southern Sudanese woman and her fifteen-year-old son. The mother says, "I used to do a lot of work, but now I have less strength, and I can only see with one eye. I want to start sewing clothes, and to save a little money each day so that my son can go to college". Her son standing beside her says, "I want to become an electrical engineer. When I see people working with electricity, I admire them and want to be like them. Then I will be able to help my family. I want to build a house for my mother and help her raise my siblings." *(Flying for the Future, magazine)*. The mother was served by missionaries, she served her son, and now his desire was to serve his mother and the rest of the family.

We are workers together in His Kingdom, and of His workers God says, *"Come, you who are blessed by my Father, inherit the Kingdom prepared for you, from the creation of the world. For I was hungry and you fed me, I was thirsty and you gave me a drink. I was a stranger, and you invited me into your home. I was naked and you clothed me. I was sick and you cared for me. I was in prison, and you visited me."* (Matthew 25:34-36).

A desire to serve God and others — was the purpose of God for those He created in His own image. However, the writer of Genesis 3:1-23 describes a catastrophic shift in humanity's allegiance.

What is commonly referred to as the "fall", was essentially humans making a choice, between serving God or following their own desires. Either they would continue to sit at His table and serve in His house, or they would sit at their own table and rule over their own house. Over time, their gratitude gave way to a sense of entitlement, and they began to seek autonomy and independence. So, when given the choice between 'being like' God — in His image, or 'as a god' — discerning between good and evil, they chose the latter. And it came at a huge cost.

The intimacy they had shared with God turned into separation from Him. Their servanthood to God, became slavery to the evil one. The assurance of eternal life became the terrible fear of judgement. Where obedience to God had once resulted in harmony and fruitfulness, disobedience led to banishment from the garden and abandonment to their own struggle for survival. The Apostle Paul puts it this way: *"When Adam sinned, sin entered the world. Adam's sin brought death, so death came to everyone for everyone sinned."*

(Romans 5:12. CJSB)

The Apostle John described the spiritual state of the world as darkness, and declared that Jesus was the light of humankind ... *"The light shines in the darkness, and the darkness has not suppressed it."* (John 1:5. CJSB)

Humanity's capacity for unconditional love along with enduring and meaningful relationships was severely damaged on that fateful day. But something else happened in the garden. Adam's decision unleashed an alternative way of living for humans. Instead of a lifestyle based on gratitude, humility and love for God and others — this lifestyle would be driven by a desire to fulfill personal needs and to put worship of self and self-determination above everything else.

Only one Man could and would bring healing and restoration of all that Adam and Eve had lost, including reconciliation with the Father. His name is Jesus!

For Further Study

Read Genesis 1:26-31 and compare it with Genesis 3:1-23. Reflect on the wonder of God creating everything and especially humankind.

Reflect on the quality of the relationship between God and humankind. Harmony, joy, peace. What really happened when man shifted their allegiance? Read Romans 5:12-21.

What do you consider are some of the differences between 'being like God' and 'being as a god'?

Chapter Three

Servanthood in the Old Testament

CHAPTER THREE

SERVANTHOOD IN THE OLD TESTAMENT

JACOB:

Shameless, Shifty, Liar and Supplanter ... to Selfless Servant and Father of Israel.

"God appeared to Jacob again when he came from Paddan Aram and blessed him. God said to him, 'Your name is Jacob; no longer shall your name be called Jacob, but Israel shall be your name. So, he called his name Israel. And God said to him, 'I am almighty God, be fruitful and multiply. A nation and a company of nations shall come from you, and kings shall come from your own body. The land that I gave Abraham and Isaac I will give to you, and I will give the land to your offspring after you".

(Genesis 35:9-15).

Jacob, whose name means 'supplanter': someone who takes another's place, often through cunning, deceit, or by seizing an opportunity — is an amazing example of a man transformed by the power and love of God. Jacob is changed from being a supplanter ... to one, who in his mature manhood demonstrated humility, repentance and love. He became a revered and effective leader with a new name, 'Israel' — which means 'contender or wrestler with God'.

Jacob's dream at Bethel and his wrestling-with-God experience, are pivotal encounters where he experiences God's presence and power. These encounters transformed Jacob from being a self-focused individual, to someone who recognized his role as a servant in God's plan.

Jacob's transformed life was no longer just about personal gain. God's promises to him included being a blessing to all peoples. His descendants became the twelve tribes of Israel, fulfilling God's plan to bless the world through service and faithfulness. Jacob's reconciliation with Esau after years of estrangement is a powerful act of humility and servanthood. He approaches Esau with gifts and respect, seeking restoration and peace, rather than asserting his dominance.

Jacob's story told primarily in Genesis ... from chapters 25 to 50 ... sets a pattern for future generations. His transformation, service, and faithfulness become foundational for the nation of Israel — illustrating that true greatness in God's eyes comes through serving others, obeying God's will and living by faith.

Jacob's life moves from self-interest and striving, to humility, and dependence on God. His story shows that biblical servanthood is about trusting God, serving others, seeking reconciliation and leaving a legacy of faith and service.

During our many years of ministry we have been deeply impressed by people whose academic ability and training, skills and life experience were much greater than ours, and yet they were content to join teams where *we* had the leadership responsibility. They sought no favours, nor did they flaunt their superior knowledge and experience. They were true servants simply seeking to continue serving others as they had done all their lives.

Moses:

God's Faithful Servant. Israel's Greatest Leader.

Another example of a humble leader is Moses — born in humble circumstances, raised in Pharaoh's household, yet later fleeing Egypt after defending a fellow Hebrew by killing his Egyptian tormentor. During his flight, Moses was startled one day to see a bush in the desert burning but not being consumed. Drawn to this phenomenon, he was further astonished when God spoke to him.

God spoke to Moses from the burning bush, not because of his status or eloquence, but because of his willingness to obey and serve. He stands as a powerful example to all church leaders today whether we are pastors or team members. Leading with humility, as Moses did, means recognising that leadership is about serving God and others, not seeking personal recognition and power.

Moses repeatedly demonstrated obedience to God's commands, even when he felt inadequate or afraid. He intentionally sought to know God's will. He depended on God for guidance, strength, and wisdom, especially when leading the Israelites out of Egypt and through the wilderness. He demonstrated that as leaders of teams and pastors of congregations, we should prioritise prayer, seeking God's wisdom for decisions and relying on His strength rather than our own abilities.

Moses sacrificed personal comfort and safety to serve God's people. He interceded for the Israelites, often putting their needs above his own, even pleading with God to forgive them after they'd sinned. As his story unfolds, Moses gradually moves from being a reluctant leader of a people eager to escape Egypt. Even though they were quick to complain when events did not unfold as they hoped, he becomes a leader convinced that God was in control of Israel's destiny.

As pastors and church leaders today, we frequently find ourselves on the same learning curve as Moses. Often, the people we minister to are initially excited about the vision God gives, but when difficulties arise, that excitement can turn to negativity and even non-cooperation. At the same time, we may become more convinced than ever that this is the path God has called us to walk.

The courage and perseverance we need at these times comes to us, as it did for Moses, from God. Moses is described as *"very humble, more than anyone else on the face of the earth"* (Numbers 12:3). And in Deuteronomy 34:10-12 we read, *"There has never been another prophet in Israel like Moses, whom the Lord knew face to face. The Lord sent him to perform all the miraculous signs and wonders in the land of Egypt against Pharoah, and all his servants, and his entire land. With mighty power, Moses performed terrifying acts in the sight of all Israel."*

His humility allowed him to be teachable, to accept correction, and to put God's will and the people's welfare above his own pride.

These days, we spend a lot of time and energy in this season of our lives encouraging young men and women, who aspire to some form of leadership, be it in the Church or elsewhere. We advise them to have the humility that allows them to seek out mentors, and to make regular mentoring a building block for growth throughout their whole life. This means that in the spirit of teachability, they are inviting someone to challenge and sometimes correct them, as well as to be accountable.

Despite opposition, constant complaints, and many personal challenges, Moses remained faithful to his calling. He had good reasons many times to quit or resign, but he persevered in serving God and the Israelites for forty years, demonstrating that servanthood often requires endurance.

Moses regularly acted as a mediator between God and the Israelites, indicating that servanthood includes advocating for others. The most important role a leader can perform, is to appoint a group of intercessors that they can rely on to pray for them, while at the same time dedicating much of their own time to praying for the people in their care.

During the forty years in the wilderness, Moses was increasingly sharing his leadership role with a man called Joshua, who was to become one of Israel's greatest servant leaders.

Joshua:

From faithful followership to servant-leadership.

Joshua began as Moses' assistant, serving faithfully for years before becoming the leader of Israel. Moses was his mentor, and Joshua learned by observing and supporting Moses, demonstrating that servant leadership often starts with humble service and learning from others. His leadership was marked by strict obedience to God's instructions, whether it was in crossing the Jordan, conquering Jericho, or in the dividing up of the promised land among the tribes.

When servant leaders prioritize God's will above personal ambition or popular opinion, they step into 'rare air'. It is not easy and sometimes not understood by others, especially those who value tradition above walking and serving by faith.

Joshua demonstrated courage in the face of daunting challenges, trusting God's promises even when circumstances seemed impossible. Servant leaders inspire others by their faith and willingness to step out in trust. This was powerfully demonstrated when the time came to take the promised land.

God had told Joshua to abandon the traditional military approach and command the people of Israel to march around the city of Jericho once a day for six days. On the seventh day, they were to march around it seven times. Then after they had completed the seventh circuit, the priests were to blow their ram horns ... the people were to give a mighty shout then the walls would collapse.

Sounds crazy? Yes, it does! ... but the point is that God told him to do it and that is just what he did.

Joshua delegated responsibilities, such as appointing leaders for each tribe and encouraging the people to claim their inheritance. Servant leadership involves empowering others to fulfill their God-given roles. Listen as he speaks to the people at the end of his life, in Joshua 23:2-3. *"I am now a very old man. You have seen everything the Lord your God has done for you in my lifetime. The Lord your God has fought for you against your enemies."*

Then at the very end of the book of Joshua we read these words. *"Then Joshua died at the age of one hundred and ten ... The people of Israel served the Lord throughout the lifetime of Joshua and of the Elders who outlived him — those who had personally experienced all that the Lord had done for Israel."* (Joshua 24:29;31).

He constantly reminded the Israelites of their covenant with God, and the importance of serving Him alone. When servant leaders build community by leading out of their own 'experience of seeing all the things the Lord has done,' it becomes evident that the authority of their leadership comes from the depth of their own personal commitment to the Lord's purposes.

For Further Study

As you consider Jacob's story, what spiritual encounters have you had in your journey that have radically changed your life?

What character qualities did Joseph demonstrate despite being sold by his brothers and being falsely accused and imprisoned? How does the answer to this question help you in your approach to the challenges you face?

Moses was described as "very humble, more than anyone else on the face of the earth." In what ways did this great leader demonstrate humility?

It was Joshua, not Moses, who was chosen to lead Israel into the promised land. Read Joshua Chapters 3-6. What qualities of leadership did he demonstrate when he led the people across the Jordan, and when he obeyed God in relation to the defeat of Jericho?

Chapter Four

The Promised Servant

CHAPTER FOUR

THE PROMISED SERVANT

The Old Testament Scriptures provide a rich tapestry of references which highlight the coming of Jesus as the ultimate servant, particularly in the writings of Isaiah.

1. The Suffering Servant in Isaiah:

Isaiah 42:1-9: *"Here is my servant whom I have chosen, the one I love, in whom I delight; I will put my Spirit on him, and he will proclaim justice to the nations. He will not quarrel or cry out: no one will hear his voice in the streets. A bruised reed he will not break and a smouldering wick he will not snuff out till he has brought justice through to victory. In his name the nations will put their hope."*

Isaiah prophesies that in due time, God is sending a Messiah, who would come as a servant, who is gentle, compassionate and powerful. On whom He has placed His Spirit. He has been chosen, and he is loved by God. He will preach justice to the nations and to all who have been wronged.

In Isaiah 49:1-7, the Prophet tells us that the Servant who is to come is called by God from the womb to be a 'light to the Gentiles'. Furthermore, in his gospel Luke reports the words of the elderly rabbi Simeon, as he held the baby Jesus in his arms. *"Sovereign Lord, now let your servant die in peace as you have promised. I have seen your salvation which you have prepared for all people. He is a light to reveal God to the nations, and he is the glory of your people Israel."* (Luke 2:30-32).

Isaiah 50:4-11, portrays the Servant as a teacher who sustains the weary with wisdom willingly enduring suffering and humiliation. *"The Sovereign Lord has given me his words of wisdom so that I will know how to comfort the weary."* (verse 4*). "The Sovereign Lord has spoken to me, and I have listened. I have not rebelled or turned away."* (verse 5). *"I offered my back to those who beat me and my cheeks to those who pulled out my beard. I did not hide my face from mockery and spitting."* (verse 6).

Isaiah 52:13–53:12 describes the Servant's suffering and ultimate sacrifice — bearing the sins of many and bringing healing and redemption. *"But he was pierced for our rebellion, crushed for our sins. He was beaten so we could be whole. He was whipped so we could be healed. All of us, like sheep have strayed away. We have left God's paths and followed our own. Yet the Lord has laid on him the sins of us all."* (NLT).

Let's be clear: Jesus did not come to Earth as a victim — He was *never* at the mercy of others. He came as God in human form, fully possessing divine authority. No power in the universe could take His life from Him. Instead, Jesus willingly offered Himself as a sacrifice for sin, so that those who had turned away from God could be forgiven. For a long time, the diluting or softening of this truth — in order to make it more acceptable — has caused significant harm to the Church.

As a child, Jesus grew up in a Jewish home and learnt the Torah, as well as the prophetic scriptures. He was well acquainted with them, yet he also possessed a deep understanding of his Father, God and recognized that the prophetic scriptures referred to him. He *was* the suffering Servant! And the eternal salvation of humankind, depended on *his* absolute obedience, love, humility and faithfulness.

One of the great narratives in the Bible is the announcement of the Messiah's coming. This event was foretold by Isaiah and other prophets centuries in advance, and when the time was right, it was also communicated through angelic messengers and extraordinary occurrences to the principal individuals involved. This is how it unfolded:

ZECHARIAH:

Zechariah, a priest of Israel was on duty in the Temple when he was startled by an angel named Gabriel. Gabriel told him that despite their old age, he and his wife Elizabeth were going to give birth to a son, whom they would name John. John would become a prophet, great in the eyes of the Lord, who, filled with the Holy Spirit, would minister powerfully, in the likeness of Elijah. He would be known as John the Baptist. John would herald the coming of the Messiah, and he would one day baptize Jesus and declare to his own disciples: *"Behold, the Lamb of God, who takes away the sin of the world"*. (John 1:29).

In Luke 1: 17 Gabriel is quoted as declaring the words of the prophet Malachi: *"He will prepare the people for the coming of the Lord. He will turn the hearts of the fathers to the children, and he will cause those who are rebellious to accept the wisdom of the godly."*

MARY:

Mary was a sixteen-year-old girl living in Nazareth and looking forward to her marriage to Joseph, a local carpenter. An angelic visit was the last thing on her mind, especially one that informed her that she — a virgin — was about to conceive and give birth to a baby boy. Gabriel not only explained what she would call her son, he also revealed the kind of person Jesus would grow up to be. *"He will be very great and will be called the Son of the Most High. The Lord God will give Him the throne of His ancestor David. And He will reign over Israel forever; His Kingdom will never end"* (Luke 1:32-33).

Shocked and confused Mary asked Gabriel, *"How can this be? I am a virgin."* He then told her, *"The Holy Spirit will come upon you, and the power of the most high will overshadow you. So, the baby to be born will be holy and He will be called the Son of God."*

(Luke 1:34-35 NLT)

JOSEPH:

An angel also appeared to Joseph, the man Mary was to marry. The angel told him, *"Joseph, son of David, don't be afraid to take Mary to be your wife. For, the child within her was conceived by the Holy Spirit. She will have a son, and you are to name him Jesus, for he will save His people from their sins"* (Matthew 1:20-21).

THE SHEPHERDS:

The night when Jesus was born, shepherds were surprised by an angel's appearance. This was not the sort of thing that happened every night. They would be even more surprised when they realised they were among the first to hear the news the angel brought. *"Don't be afraid. I bring you good news that will bring great joy to all people. The Saviour — yes, the Messiah, the Lord — has been born today in Bethlehem. And you will recognise him by this sign. You will find a baby wrapped snugly in strips of cloth, lying in a manger."* Luke 2:10-12. (NLT)

THE WISE MEN AND HEROD:

King Herod would have been bemused by an unexpected visit by a bunch of eastern academics who had followed an unusual star to Jerusalem. His bemusement, however, quickly turned to anger, when they explained that the star indicated that a long-awaited King of the Jews had been born. A quick discussion with his own priests, disclosed that the faithful believed that one day the coming King — the Messiah — would be born in Bethlehem.

"And you, O Bethlehem in the land of Judah are not least among the cities of Judah, for a ruler will come from you, who will be the shepherd for my people Israel."
(Matthew 2:6 NLT)

Herod immediately began planning the demise of this so-called king. This news was so convincing and devastating that he later ordered the death of every boy under two years old, born in Bethlehem.

For Further Study

More than 400 years before Jesus was born, Isaiah spoke of His birth, His ministry and His death. Read Isaiah 42:1-9. Write down and meditate on each of the descriptive statements used of Jesus.

One of the descriptive statements in 42:1 is that the one who is to come is the 'chosen servant'. Isaiah 50:4 calls him the 'obedient servant and Isaiah 52:13 calls Him 'the suffering servant.' Compare these passages with Philippians 2:5-8.

When the angel visits Mary (Luke 1:26-38) and Joseph (Matthew 1:20-23) and the Shepherds (Luke 2:8-14) what descriptive words were used of Jesus?

Chapter Five

Old Testament Servants

CHAPTER FIVE

JESUS – THE ULTIMATE SERVANT

He was the most powerful, the best connected, the most capable and the most knowledgeable person ever to live on earth. Yet, he chose to come as a servant and to model an alternative way of life to the rest of the world. We call it ... SERVANTHOOD.

His birth was remarkable. Promised to a young woman — engaged but not yet married and living in the truly insignificant town of Nazareth — he was conceived by the power of the Holy Spirit and ultimately born in a stable in Bethlehem, where his first bed was a cattle feed trough. Among his first visitors were some rough shepherds to whom God had announced the birth of the one who was to become their Saviour. A King? Yes! The Almighty God who became human? Yes! The Supreme Servant? Yes!

On one amazing occasion when Jesus the Messiah, the Son of the living God, was twelve years old, for a short time He was lost in Jerusalem by his earthly parents, Joseph and Mary. When the distraught couple found Him, he was in the temple talking to the teachers about the Scriptures. Jesus seemed surprised that they were worried: *"Did you not know that I must be about my Fathers business?"* he enquired. (Luke 2:49 Douay-Rheims Bible)

The next time we hear about Jesus is eighteen years later. Matthew tells us in his Gospel that Jesus arrives one day at the Jordan River where John the Baptist is baptizing those who are repenting of their sins. Jesus asks John to baptize him and John — fully aware that Jesus is the Messiah — protests, *"I am the one who needs to be baptised by you. Why are you coming to me?"* To which Jesus replies, *"It should be done, for we must carry out all that God requires."* (Matthew 3:13-14)

Matthew then tells us that as Jesus came out of the water. *"...the heavens were opened, and John saw the Spirit of God descending like a dove and settling on him. And a voice from heaven* said, *"This is my beloved Son, who brings me great joy."* (Matthew 3:15-17).

Son of God!? Yes!

Servant of God doing what God requires? Most assuredly ... Yes!

Think about it this way. Here at the river Jordan stand two of the most significant figures of all time. One of them, John the Baptist, insists that he is not worthy to untie the sandals of the other, Jesus, who has asked him to baptize him. Speaking of Jesus, John said, *"This is the one I was talking about when I said, 'Someone is coming after me who is greater than I am, for He existed long before I did."*

(John 1:15 TLB).

Of John, Jesus said. *"I tell you the truth. Of all who have ever lived, none is greater than John the Baptist. Yet even the least person in the Kingdom of Heaven is greater than he is."* (Matthew 11:11) Two leaders scratching each other's backs? I think not. Rather, two servants demonstrating what it means to live in humility, submitting to and honouring one another.

The Gospel writer Luke, tells us that immediately after His baptism, Jesus allowed Himself to be led by the devil into the wilderness. Jesus knew that it was the Father's will that he be tempted in the same way as we are. And he was, without yielding to the temptations he faced. No wonder John the Baptist could cry out:

> *"From His abundance we have all received one gracious blessing after another. For the law was given through Moses, but God's unfailing love and faithfulness came through Jesus Christ."*
>
> (John 1:16-17).

On another significant occasion, Jesus demonstrated servanthood by washing his disciples' feet.

> *"Do you understand what I was doing. You call me 'Teacher' and 'Lord', and you are right, because that is what I am. And since I, your Lord and Teacher, have washed your feet, you ought to wash each other's feet. I have given you an example to follow. Do as I have done to you. I tell you the truth, slaves are not greater than their master. Nor is the messenger greater than the one who sends the message. Now that you know these things, God will bless you for doing them."*
>
> (John 13:12-17).

Teacher? Yes! Lord? Yes!

The One who sends the Message? No!

He is the Message —the Word — sent from the Father.

We now come to a key teaching of Jesus found in Matthew 20: 25-18. "*Jesus called the disciples together and said, "You know that the rulers of this world lord it over their people, and officials flaunt their authority over those under them. But among you it will be different. Whoever wants to be a leader among you must be your servant and whoever wants to be first among you must become your slave. For even the Son of Man came not to be* served *but to serve others and to give his life a ransom for many."*

Here, Jesus draws a contrast between the leadership model used by the rulers and officials of their world and what would be expected of his disciples. In describing the 'rulers of this world', Jesus uses two powerful expressions that convey the concept of superiority and power ... 'lord it over' and 'flaunt their authority.' He tells them that the style of leadership in his Kingdom will be the opposite to the one the rulers of this world follow. "*But among you it will be different.*" Leadership will not be about lording it over those we lead or using authority to meet our needs for recognition and achievement. It will be about serving.

It is important to remember that there was nothing weak or indecisive about the leadership demonstrated by Moses, Joshua or Jesus. The point is that their authority was rooted in their integrity as servants of God who honoured and loved those they led.

This would have been confusing to the disciples. Every style of leadership they had experienced in their lives, whether it had been the power and authority of their Roman occupiers, or the pomp and power of the Pharisees, was built on pride and fear.

During the first year of his ministry, Jesus modelled both life and leadership to his disciples. They were learning what his priorities were, and he urged them to make *his* priorities *theirs*. His priority was to speak the words he heard the Father speak and do the works the Father gave him to do.

In the Gospels we find Jesus at the Jordan river for his baptism, then in the wilderness being tempted by the devil; then by the lake of Galilee calling men to follow him; then on a mountainside teaching his disciples. He fed five thousand people with a boy's lunch ... calmed a mighty storm on the lake and debated with the Pharisees and the Sadducees in Jerusalem ... healed and delivered people in Capernaum and the region of the Gadarenes and declared that he was the Messiah to a Samaritan woman. He foretold his death and resurrection and demonstrated what it meant to trust explicitly in the Father and the Holy Spirit. In every aspect of his life, we see the Holy Spirit at work.

He was:

Conceived by the Holy Spirit — Luke 1:35.

Anointed by the Spirit — Luke 4:18; Acts 10:38; Isaiah 61:1.

Filled with the Holy Spirit — Luke 4:1;14. John 3:34.

Sealed by the Holy Spirit —John 6:27.

Led by the Spirit — Luke 4:1.

Rejoiced in the Spirit — Luke 10:21.

Gave commands by the Spirit — Acts 1:2.

Performed miracles by the power of the Spirit — Matthew 12:28; Luke 4:14-15,18.

Resurrected by the Spirit — Romans 8:11.

Promised his disciples that they would receive **the Holy Spirit** after he had ascended into heaven — Luke 24:49.

THE CROSS: SERVICE AND SACRIFICE

We have already seen that Isaiah spoke of Jesus as the Suffering Servant. Jesus, in John 10:11 seems to take same theme:

> *"I am the good shepherd; I know my own sheep, and they know me, just as my father knows me and I know the father. So, I sacrifice my life for the sheep, I have other sheep, too, that are not in this sheepfold. I must bring them also. They will listen to my voice and there will be one flock with one shepherd.*
>
> *"The Father loves me because I sacrifice my life so I may take it back again. No one can take my life from me. I sacrifice it voluntarily. For I have the authority to lay it down when I want to and to take it up again. For this is what my Father commanded."*

Laying down His life voluntarily was always the divine

plan. We have already seen that this was revealed to Isaiah and recorded some four hundred years before the birth of Jesus. It was later revealed to John the Baptist, who declared to those who would become Jesus' disciples, *"Behold, the Lamb of God who takes away the sin of the world."*

Jesus also spoke of his voluntary death at the Last Supper, when He broke the bread, saying: *" 'This is my body which is given for you." And when He shared the cup saying, "This is my blood of the new covenant which is poured out for many.' "* (Mark 14:22-25).

When we follow Jesus to the Garden of Gethsemane in Luke 22:39-46, and listen to the prayer he prayed, we are convinced that what was about to happen would require his absolute obedience. *"Father if you are willing, please take this cup of suffering away from Me. Yet I want your will to be done, not mine. Then an angel from heaven appeared and strengthened Him. He prayed more fervently, and he was in such agony of spirit that his sweat fell to the ground like great drops of blood."* (42-44).

In the Roman judgement hall, Pilate says to Jesus, *"Don't you realise I have the power to release you or crucify you?"* to which Jesus replies, *"You would have no power over me at all unless it were given to you from above."* (John 19:10-11).

Yes, indeed Jesus was and is the ultimate servant and even today he is ready for when the Father says that it is time to come for His Church and to establish his eternal Kingdom.

For Further Study

When it comes to servant leadership Matthew 20:24-28 is a key passage. How do you understand what Jesus is saying when He contrasts leadership in Gods Kingdom with leadership in the secular and religious world?

How would a leader "Lord it over their people" and 'flaunt their authority? What might it look like?

In what ways do you think we can serve those we may be called to lead?

What are we actually doing when we seek to be 'first' among others?

What is the significance in Jesus using himself as both a model of leadership and a model of servanthood?

Chapter Six

Walking in the Spirit of Servanthood

CHAPTER SIX

WALKING IN THE SPIRIT OF SERVANTHOOD

The truth that Jesus walked in the power of the Holy Spirit, and that he promised his disciples that they would receive the Holy Spirit after His resurrection and ascension, is vital to any discussion about servanthood. The miracles he performed ... the wisdom he shared ... the humility he modelled ... and his unwavering obedience to the will of his Father, were all part of the evidence that he was the Messiah. He alone had the authority to declare that one day the disciples would be indwelt by the same Spirit, have access to the same power and wisdom, and walk in the same humility and obedience he had demonstrated.

When Paul instructed new Christians in Galatia to walk in the Spirit, his teaching was profound. First, he tells them that if we let the Holy Spirit guide our lives, we will not be doing what our sinful nature desires. Indeed, the Spirit gives us desires that are the opposite to those of the sinful nature. These two forces are constantly at war with each other. *"When you follow the desires of the sinful nature, the results are very clear: sexual immorality, impurity, lustful pleasures, idolatry, sorcery, hostility, quarrelling, jealousy, outbursts of anger, selfish ambition, dissension, division, envy, drunkenness, wild parties and other sins like these."* (Galatians 5:19-21).

Then in verses 22-23, Paul tells us what our lives will produce if we walk in the Spirit. *"But the Holy Spirit produces this kind of fruit in our lives: love, joy, peace, patience, kindness, goodness, faithfulness, gentleness and self-control. There is no law against these things."*

LOVE ... of God ... ourselves ... our families ... our neighbours ... strangers ... our congregations and even our enemies.

> *"Love is patient and kind. Love is not jealous or rude. It does not demand its own way. It is not irritable, and it keeps no record of being wronged. It does not rejoice about injustice but rejoices whenever the truth wins out. Love never gives up, never loses faith, is always hopeful, and endures through every circumstance."* (1Corinthians 13:4-7).

Love is a gift that releases us from self-centredness and empowers us to serve others without any guarantee of a reward.

JOY ... is a deep, enduring sense of well-being and contentment that comes from our relationship with God. It is a character quality that can be present even during our greatest trials and it is the fruit of an attitude that trusts in God's goodness and faithfulness. Joy is the fruit of the Spirit that constantly rewards us for our service toward others.

PEACE ... in a biblical context transcends a simple absence of conflict. It encompasses wholeness, restoration, and a deep sense of well-being rooted in our relationship with God. Jesus said, *"I am leaving you with a gift — peace of mind and heart. And the peace I give is a gift the world cannot give. So do not be troubled or afraid."* (John 14:27 NLT).

Peace is the fruit of the Spirit that enables us to remain calm in the storms of life, while others are afraid.

PATIENCE ... is a powerful and multifaceted virtue ... revealed in endurance and forbearance, grounded in trust in God's timing, and expressed through love, acceptance, and forgiveness. *"Since God chose you, to be the holy people he loves, you must clothe yourselves with tender-hearted mercy, kindness, humility, gentleness and patience."* (Colossians 3:12).

Patience is the fruit of the Spirit that guarantees that the needs of those we serve will always be more important than ours.

KINDNESS ... involves selfless acts of generosity, forgiveness and empathy, even toward those who are difficult or undeserving. Talking about kindness to his disciples Jesus said, *"Love your enemies! Do good to them. Lend to them without expecting to be repaid. Then your reward from heaven will be very great and you will be truly acting as children of the Most High, for He is kind to those who are unthankful and wicked. You must be compassionate, just as your Father is compassionate."*
(Luke 16:35-36).

Kindness is the fruit of the Spirit that generates service to others.

GOODNESS ... is about reflecting God's nature and will to the world, knowing that our salvation and reconciliation to Him is the outcome of His goodness toward us. The goodness of God is the cornerstone of our salvation. *"For God loved the world so much that He gave His only Son, so that everyone who believes in Him will not perish but have eternal life. God sent His Son into the world not to judge the world, but to save the world through Him."* (John 3:16-17).

Goodness is the fruit of the Spirit that influences the ethical aspect of our service to others.

FAITHFULNESS ... in the Bible, refers to both God's faithfulness, truthfulness and unchanging nature, and His call and empowerment of us to reflect that faithfulness in our lives. *"I will sing of the Lord's unfailing love forever! Young and old will hear of your faithfulness. Your unfailing love will last forever. Your faithfulness is as enduring as the heavens."* (Psalms 89:1-2).

Being faithful to God and trusting in his faithfulness, is the fruit of the Spirit that ensures the longevity of our service to others.

GENTLENESS ... often linked with meekness, and humility. It is a mild, tender and considerate nature, not a weakness, but a controlled strength and a Christlike disposition that reflects God's character and the influence of the Holy Spirit in our lives. *"Then Jesus said, 'Come to me all of you who carry heavy burdens, and I will give you rest. Take my yoke upon you. Let me teach you, because I am humble and gentle at heart and you will find rest for your souls."* (Matthew 11:28).

The fruit of gentleness influences the character of our service to others.

SELF-CONTROL ... is the God given ability to regulate one's thoughts, emotions and actions, aligning them with Gods will. *"In view of all this make every effort to respond to God's promises. Supplement faith, with a generous provision of moral excellence, and moral excellence with knowledge, and knowledge with self-control, and self-control with patient endurance, and patient endurance with godliness, and godliness with brotherly affection, and brotherly affection with love for everyone."* (2 Peter 1:5-9).

Self-control is the fruit of the Spirit that most influences the consistency of our service.

Each of these nine virtues is clearly seen in the life of Jesus. Together, they are evidence of the presence and power of the Holy Spirit and the primary reason we should imitate Him.

The Apostle Paul, more than any other New Testament writer, wrote about the servant heart of Jesus and why it is important for us to be impacted and influenced by it. When writing to the new believers in Philippi, Paul encourages them to live as God had ordained them to. He tells them that if they have been encouraged by discovering that they now belong to Christ; and if they have been comforted by his love and if they feel united in fellowship with each other — then:

> *"Make me truly happy by agreeing wholeheartedly with each other, loving one another, gathering with one mind and purpose. Don't be selfish. Don't try to impress others. Be humble and think of others better than you think of yourselves. Don't look out only for your own interests but take an interest in others too. You must have the same attitude that Christ Jesus had. Though he was God, he did not think of equality with God as something to cling to. Instead, he gave up his divine privileges; he took the humble position of a servant and was born as a human being. When he appeared in human form, he humbled himself in obedience to God and died a criminal's death on a cross."* (Philippians 2:5-8).

When you look at the man Jesus, what do you see?

A man of authority and power?

A man with rights and privileges, riches and prestige?

No!

We see a man who laid all that down and took a position comparable to that of a servant — right at the bottom of the social scale. A man who, at thirty-three years of age, would experience the ignominy, suffering, and pain of a criminal's death, although he had committed no crime.

All this leads us to ask the all-important question: What does the example and teaching of Jesus, the head of the Church — His body, and the Apostle Paul teach us about modern day Church Leadership?

For Further Study

Read Galatians 5:16-26.

Paul names nine fruit of the Spirit. They are listed here for you to reflect on and to write comments that indicate how they particularly relate to you.

Love …

Joy …

Peace …

Patience …

Kindness …

Goodness …

Faithfulness …

Gentleness …

Self-Control …

To help get you started, ask yourself the question: *in what ways does my choice to walk or not to walk in the Spirit impact those close to me or those I lead?*

Reflect on Galatians 5:13. *"For you have been called to freedom my brothers and sisters. But don't use your freedom to satisfy your sinful nature. Instead use your freedom to serve one another in love."*

Chapter Seven

FORMED by the SPIRIT to SERVE

CHAPTER SEVEN

FORMED BY THE SPIRIT TO SERVE

It is important to understand that whilst the fruit of the Spirit can be produced in the life of any and every believer, it is always the result of "walking" in the Spirit. Fruit-bearing leaders are those who choose to walk in the Spirit. That choice places them in a position where they lead, not in the spirit of emperors, kings, prime ministers, presidents, and dictators, but in the Spirit of Christ. Their character and their various leadership styles are refined, influenced and empowered by the Holy Spirit.

As a young Christian preparing for ministry, I (Graeme) was greatly influenced and inspired by the life and leadership of the highly respected evangelist Dr. Billy Graham. In 1959 and 1968-69 he visited Australia for two great evangelistic crusades. The 1959 Crusade, being the highlight, resulted in an attendance of over 3 million, with the final meeting at the Melbourne Cricket Ground attracting a record crowd of 143,750 people. We had the privilege of being there and witnessing thousands choosing to become followers of Christ. Servant leadership was evident in every aspect of Dr. Graham's life and ministry. He often spent long periods away from his family, traveling extensively to preach the Gospel. He desperately missed his wife Ruth and his young family, and naturally, they missed him too. Despite this and many others challenges, he remained dedicated to his mission throughout his whole life, demonstrating his commitment to serving Christ and others.

Throughout his ministry, Dr. Graham maintained a reputation for integrity and humility. He avoided scandals and controversies, focusing on his mission to preach the Gospel. His humble demeanor and genuine care for people earned him respect and trust. Before each of his crusades he and his team would train thousands of counsellors, recruited from participating churches. He was insistent that every person who responded to the appeal to accept Christ was counselled, prayed for and connected to a local congregation.

Billy Graham worked to unite Christians across denominational lines. He collaborated with various Christian leaders and organizations, promoting unity within the body of Christ in every city he ministered in. In Australia in 1959 such unity between different denominations and Christian organizations was almost unheard of and it was a powerful witness to the wider community.

He was known for his strong moral and ethical stance. He spoke out on social issues, advocating for justice, peace, and righteousness. His messages often addressed the moral challenges of the times, encouraging people to live according to biblical principles. He not only opposed racial segregation but insisted on racial integration in his crusades. In 1957 he invited Martin Luther King to speak at one of his crusade meetings in New York.

His whole life and ministry was an example of servant leadership in action. He often emphasized the importance of humility and service as a reflection of the life style set by Jesus Christ.

One of the characteristics of his ministry, was that he was surrounded by a large team and each of them flourished in their own way. Cliff Burroughs — song leader and choir director, George Beverley Shea — gospel singer and hymn composer, Grady Wilson — associate evangelist and Vice President of the Billy Graham Association. Many others were all as well known and as greatly loved as Billy Graham himself.

The ministry of the Billy Graham Organisation was not the result of a man sitting in the director's chair orchestrating every administrative move and making every organisational decision. Instead, it resulted from a large group of men and women who chose to walk in the Spirit together. The wide range of administrative and management skills that emerged as they were needed: preaching and training abilities that were required ... music ... literature ... film and television capabilities all rose from a community of people who loved God, who loved the world in which they ministered and who chose to walk in the Spirit.

When, as leaders, we obey the call to follow Christ we are accepting an invitation to imitate him and his demonstration of servanthood. In a very real sense however, it is much more than that. Receiving him into our lives in the person of the Holy Spirit, means that we have the potential of being empowered to be like him, in our love, joy, peace, patience, kindness, goodness, faithfulness, gentleness, and self-control.

When Graeme was a young pastor, a godly mentor spoke into his life about preaching. He said, "Graeme, every time you stand up to preach, ask God to help you love every person in the congregation, more than you love preaching." This statement had a strong impact on his ministry and praying that prayer became something he has done ever since then whether he is preaching to a congregation or speaking at a Rotary Club or school.

It is easy to be seduced by the power and privilege of preaching, and the adrenalin hit that comes from displaying your theological and doctrinal knowledge and to "preach at the people." On the other hand, the result of loving the congregation more than preaching, is that you "preach *for* the people." You preach for their salvation, for their spiritual growth, for their healing and for the purpose of strengthening their call to mission.

We also found that a meaningful way to 'love on' the congregation, was to go to the door and greet everybody as they left the Church. When we served a congregation of several hundred, there were two exit doors, and so we would take a door each. We got to know everybody by name, meet new people and hear what was happening in people's lives. Much of our pastoral care during the following week was a response to what we heard at the door.

When we preach, the congregation should feel pastored, shepherded and enriched as well as challenged and if needed, convicted of their need for change. But they should never feel unloved, harangued or misunderstood. When we love our congregation more than we love preaching, the Holy Spirit is free to work through this loving servant attitude, and bring encouragement, growth and change into the hearts of those who hear us.

Graeme shares the next story about a formational event in his own life. "When I became a pastor, at the age of twenty, I was not only inexperienced and immature, but I was 'full of myself'. By the grace of God many things happened that challenged my self-focus. The lessons I learnt through these events and encounters not only affected me at the time but are still cornerstones of my understanding and practise of ministry. Let me tell you one of these stories.

The Church I pastored was in a country town in northeastern Victoria. During the two years I was there, we decided to have a special evangelistic outreach one weekend. This was the largest event that I had ever organised. I was consumed with all that needed to be done. And then … the letter arrived.

It was from a lady called Marjorie who told me that she and her husband were planning to be in the town on the same weekend of our event. She explained that she had relatives in the town whom she had not seen for decades and did not know their address. She asked me if I would look them up with the hope that they could stay with them before continuing their trip.

I am ashamed now to tell you that I was very ungracious. The nerve of these people asking this of me. Didn't they know I was busy with more important things? I did however look up their relatives and discovered they were nominal Catholics and people of the world and were not at all interested in a visit from these folk. They even requested that I not give Marjorie their address.

I remained ungracious, complaining about these thoughtless people who had put me in this position! The reality was that I lived in a three-bedroomed house on my own, so I felt obligated to invite them to stay with me. Two of the bedrooms had not even been opened in the time I had been there.

So, amid all my anxiety and busyness about the evangelistic event, I cleaned and dusted their room, made the bed and waited for their arrival. When the doorbell rang, I opened the door to one of the most wonderful couples I have ever met. Their love and joy were palpable. They sat at my kitchen table and told me their story. Marjorie had spent a large part of her life in psychiatric care. Then in her late fifties she came to know Christ, and she was miraculously healed. Somehow, she had come to own a large house in the Dandenong's and had opened it to people with mental health challenges.

Arthur, as a young Methodist minister, had become a missionary and for all his ministry had served in the Pacific Islands. During that time, he had been widowed twice and eventually returned to Melbourne, a burnt- out shell of a man. He was one of Marjorie's first residential guests. She nursed him back to physical and spiritual health, and after some time they married. And so, now together they served the people who came to stay with them.

I was so moved by their stories that I asked them to give their testimonies at the rally we were organizing for that weekend. The success of the weekend was largely due to their presence. They served the whole time they were there, cleaning, cooking and loving. They served the church like few others I had ever seen.

I was deeply blessed by these visitors I had not wanted. I had indeed 'entertained angels unawares'. Many years later Julia and I and a team of others, opened a guest house in Marysville and did much the same as Marjorie and Arthur had done. God had turned their woundedness into fruitfulness and in turn, He did the same for us.

What do you see in the people we have spoken about in this chapter and what is characteristic of all the great servant-leaders who have impacted our lives?

LOVE. Not just the belief that love is important, or the conviction that because God loved them; it was essential that they love others ... but the transformational love that flowed from the Father, to them, and then through them to others. It was the transformational love of Christ Jesus that motivated Billy Graham to take the Gospel around the world. It was the same love that transformed Marjorie so dramatically that she went from being a mental health patient to caring for people who were in the same place as she had been. It was the restoring love of Jesus that enabled Arthur to move from weakness to strength.

Listen to Paul speaking to the Corinthian Church. *"If it seems we are crazy, it is to bring glory to God. And if we are in our right minds, it is for your benefit. Either way God's love controls us. Since we believe that Christ died for all, we also believe that we have all died to our old life. He died for everyone so that those who receive His new life will no longer live for themselves. Instead, they will live for Christ, who died and was raised for them."*

(2 Corinthians 5:13-15).

God's love for us was never meant to meet only our personal needs, or simply to comfort or reassure us. It is all those things — and much, much more. It was meant to transform us: from people who lived for ourselves into people who live for God, and, like Him, have the capacity to love others more than we love ourselves. Paul continues *"So, we stopped evaluating others from a human point of view. At one time we thought of Christ merely from a human point of view. How differently we know Him now! This means that anyone who belongs to Christ, has become a new person. The old life is gone, and a new life has begun."* (2 Corinthians 5:16-17).

In Paul's experience, there was a time when he had thought of Jesus as a mere man — a carpenter from Nazareth who had gathered a large following by appearing to work amazing miracles and claiming to be the Son of God. Now, all that had changed for him. He now knew through a personal encounter with the risen Christ, that Jesus was indeed God, and that everyone who belonged to Him had been raised from spiritual death and become a new person, capable of the same humility and obedience that Jesus had demonstrated.

Paul concludes:

"And all this is a gift from God who brought us back to Himself through Christ. And God has given us this task of reconciling people to God. For God was in Christ reconciling people to Himself, no longer counting people's sins against them. And He gave us this wonderful message of reconciliation."

(2 Corinthians 5:13-19).

As the recipients of God's gift of reconciliation, our very lives were meant to be channels through which God's message of reconciliation would flow to others.

For Further Study

Take some time by yourself to write down your own transformational story.

What was happening in your life at the time when you first experienced the unconditional love of God?

How did that experience change you?

In what ways are you motivated and empowered by that same love now?

Study 2 Corinthians 5:13-15. What is Paul saying to the Christians in Corinth and more importantly what is God saying to you through this passage?

Chapter Eight

Creating a Serving Community

CHAPTER EIGHT

CREATING A SERVING COMMUNITY

When we were in our late twenties and serving as Youth Pastors, we started asking ourselves questions about the relevance and effectiveness of the local church. We loved our church. Week after week the faithful loved each other and gave attention to hearing God's Word. They loved and cared for each other but the impact on our local community was minimal. We began meeting with several other couples of a similar age, and in time our conversation turned to the Church as the Body of Christ and a community of disciples. Through an authentic, loving relationship with the Lord Jesus and a desire to serve the wider community, we came to see how believers become the channels of reconciliation Paul was speaking about.

Our discussions led to the possibility of developing a residential community. A community that actively and unconditionally invited broken and hurting people to join us and find the love, acceptance and healing that they needed. Our sense was that such people would rarely enter the doors of ours or any church and yet, what they were seeking could only come from God.

To cut a long story short, God led us to an old, dilapidated, deserted, forty-three roomed guest house in the beautiful town of Marysville, one hundred kilometres from our local church. With the help of many volunteers, we restored it to a place where it could once again function as a Guest House. We eventually felt that God was calling us to leave our home in suburban Melbourne and in 1974, with four children under twelve, we moved to Marysville and lived in two rooms at the guest house for six months, while our new house was being built next door.

To many people, the whole project was madness and doomed to fail. We had none of the skills and experience needed to run a commercial guest house and neither did the team of wonderful people that God had built around us. What the naysayers did not consider, however, was that God had called us, and we had simply obeyed.

We named the house Elkanah, which in Hebrew, means "God's possession". For the sixteen years we served there, we witnessed the most wonderful transformations in each other's lives, in the lives of those who came for healing, and in the lives of those who had been called by God to serve Him there. The original building was burnt down in the Black Saturday Bushfires of 2009, but despite this, fifty years after it all started, Elkanah still stands in Marysville, not as it was — a timber and cement sheet building — but as a stately, red brick testimony to God's faithfulness.

The very first person who came for help in the early days of our ministry there, was Norm. Norm had worked on the waterfront and one of his brothers had been murdered there. Norm was on the run because he was afraid. He was also a long-term alcoholic.

The love and acceptance he experienced, eventually opened his heart to the forgiveness and healing God was offering him, and Norm put his faith in Christ, stopped drinking, joined our team and served with us as a maintenance man for five years. God continually brought us people fleeing from domestic violence and others dealing with mental ill-health and serious relational issues, and many others like Norm were wonderfully transformed.

The point of the Elkanah story is that every staff member saw themselves as a servant. Much of our work was menial, our wages were minimal, and the hours were long, but we were grateful for being part of something God was doing. Each person had a story of how God led them to Elkanah, some as retired people, some as young people and young families … even former guests who stayed on to serve others. And each of us knew that Jesus our Master and Lord had said: *"The Son of Man did not come to be served but to serve."*

(Matthew 20:28)

One of our most significant challenges was around the issue of leadership. We understood what good leadership in a secular setting looked like, but God had called us to develop something different. We learnt that whilst the leadership style we usually develop is defined by having goals like building a successful business, making a profit, winning approval and gaining honour from what we do. Yet God had clearly called us to serve Him *and* others. That needed to remain our daily focus and the many times when our focus shifted, God would clearly and sometimes dramatically call us back.

An unplanned aspect of Elkanah's ministry began in 1980. In 1978 we had attended what was — in those days — called a Pastors and Wives Course, at the Narramore

Foundation in Los Angeles. While it was a wonderful experience for both of us, for Graeme particularly, it was these three weeks that most dramatically changed his life.

Graeme explains it in his own words:

"I was a preacher and a counsellor and as you can imagine I talked a lot about forgiveness. God's forgiveness of us and our need and obligation to forgive others. The truth was that I carried a deep wound in my spirit that I had never resolved. I had never shared my story, not even with Julia. I was deeply resentful and bitter toward a teacher who had sexually abused me as a child. The anger that I had felt about that all my life, had been internalised since I had become a Christian, at seventeen years of age. Only Julia and the children really saw it. I was secretly and deeply ashamed of the verbal anger I often poured on them. I was trapped in my own prison of internalised pain but at the same time I was pouring all my energy into helping others escape from their own prisons.

"During the course, which was primarily lectures from prominent Christian psychologists, we were required to complete several personality tests. To receive the results of those tests we needed to have a personal interview with a psychologist. When my turn came, I decided that if the tests gave him a clue to what I was struggling with, then I would tell him the whole story.

"At one point in the interview, he said to me, "I am thinking that you have two distinct parts of your life. You have a very open and public part of your life which you are happy to share and a very closed private part of your life which is hidden from everybody." He was so close to the truth, so much so, that he became the first person to hear my story. In following sessions, he patiently led me to understand the necessity of forgiving my abuser in the same way that God had forgiven me.

"When we returned to Elkanah from the USA, we felt a strong need to share what God had done in our lives with others. We began to facilitate Relationship Retreats for engaged and courting couples, Marriage Enrichment Retreats for married couples and Missionary Enrichment Retreats for missionary candidates and missionaries on furlough.

"We made the decision to make a similar course to the one we attended in Los Angeles available in Australia. In July 1980, we ran what became the first of ten annual Ministry Enrichment Retreats. Our first guest lecturer was Dr. Bruce Narramore, and each year we had prominent Christian counsellors and psychologists leading the course. We used the same personality tests, provided opportunities for personal counselling and saw pastors and their spouses from all over Australia and New Zealand benefit richly from the course.

"Our desire to serve those that God brought to us had now extended to those in national and cross-cultural ministry, as well as married and engaged couples. Many who attended these courses commented that while the teaching and counselling was helpful, the most impactful thing was the ethos and atmosphere of Elkanah.

"In recent years, people have sometimes referred to us as the former leaders of Elkanah's ministries. However, when we were there doing the work, it did not feel like leadership. Julia and I and our family were part of a living organism. A community that God had brought together to learn how to be Jesus to those in need. Together, we embraced a broad spread of gifts and skills, and we encouraged one another to trust God to take us where many of us had never ventured before."

For Further Study

We have talked in this chapter about a community of believers who set out to show Christ to those who for any reason came to live with us through loving service.

Now read Colossians 3:12-17. Study this passage and make notes about what God is specifically saying to you about how to live as Christians in the place that God has placed you.

What does Paul mean when he says, *"you must clothe yourselves with tender-hearted mercy, kindness, humility and patience"*?

Chapter Nine

Serving Others in the Early Church

CHAPTER NINE

SERVING OTHERS IN THE EARLY CHURCH

"As the believers rapidly multiplied, there were rumblings of discontent. The Greek speaking believers complained about the Hebrew speaking believers, saying that their own widows were being discriminated against in the daily distribution of food.

"So the Twelve called a meeting of all the believers. They said, 'We apostles should spend our time teaching the word of God, not running a food program. And so, brothers select seven men who are well respected and are full of the Spirit and wisdom. We will give them this responsibility. Then we apostles can spend our time in prayer and teaching the word." (Acts 6:1-4 NLT).

When the early Church in Jerusalem rapidly grew with both Jewish and Greek converts being added every day, the Greek Christians complained that their widows were being discriminated against. The Apostles understood that they had been anointed and commissioned by Jesus to preach the word, and so they directed the Church to select seven men to undertake the responsibility of organizing the care for the other needs that were arising.

What are the important elements of servant leadership we see here?

Compassion. The apostles saw the need of the Grecian widows and led the community of believers to respond to it.

Honour and respect. They honoured and respected their fellow believers and embraced them into the process of addressing the challenge together as the Body of Christ. Whatever they did to meet this challenge, there were two essential principles:

(1) The apostles must continue to be free to teach the word of God.

(2) whoever does this new work must be prayerfully chosen by the body of believers.

Humility. The Apostles understood what their part in the Body of Christ was and once they had discharged their responsibility, they stepped back and allowed the members of the Church to choose the seven deacons.

In 1 Timothy 3:1-12 Paul talks to the young church planter about local church leadership, in particular the appointing of elders and deacons. He taught Timothy that an elder and a deacon must be above reproach. They must demonstrate wisdom in their daily lives and model generosity, hospitality and faithfulness to others. They must be able to teach the Word to others, should not be heavy drinkers and should not be violent.

They should always be gentle and humble. They must manage their own family well. They must be mature so that they do not become arrogant. And they should have a good reputation in the wider community.

Listen now to Paul. *"I am writing these things to you ... so that you will know how people should conduct themselves in the household of God. This is the Church of the Living God, which is the pillar and foundation of truth."*

(1 Timothy 3:15 NLT)

He takes this concept of the Church as a household of faith and the Body of Christ further in Romans 12:4-5. *"Just as our bodies have many parts and each part has a special function, so it is with Christ's body. We are many parts of one body, and we all belong to each other."*

What he is saying is that there is another reason why servant leadership is the signature model of the Church. The first reason is that Christ modelled and commanded it, and the second is that '*we are all many parts of one body, and we belong to each other.*' We are 'one body' — not simply because we believe the same things or worship the same God — but because we have been born again by the same Spirit and been embraced by God as His children. Our willingness to serve each other and the world we live in is the evidence that we no longer belong to ourselves, but to God and His household.

Paul now introduces us to the only reason that the many members of Christ's body have the capacity to serve one another.

"In His grace, God has given us different gifts for doing certain (essential ministry functions in the Body of Christ) well. So, if God has given you the

gift of prophesy, speak out with as much faith (boldness and insight) as God has given you. If your gift is serving others, serve them well. If you are a teacher, teach (the scriptures) well. If your gift is encouraging. Encourage well. If it is giving, give generously. If God has given you leadership ability, take the responsibility seriously. And if you have a gift of showing kindness to others, do it gladly".

(Romans 12:6-8 NLT)

parentheses added

Paul teaches that spiritual gifts are exercised powerfully in the context of lives that are fiercely committed to imitating Jesus Christ. Take a few moments here to meditate on what he says in Romans 12:9-21.

"Don't just pretend to love others. Really love them. Hate what is wrong. Hold tightly to what is good. Love each other with real affection. Honor each other. Never be lazy. Work hard. Serve the Lord enthusiastically. Rejoice in the hope you have in Jesus Christ.

Be patient in trouble and keep on praying.

When God's people are in need be ready to help them.

Always be eager to practise hospitality.

Bless those who curse you, pray that God will bless them. Share happiness with the happy.

Weep with the weepers.

Live in harmony with each other

Don't be too proud to enjoy the company of ordinary people.

Don't think you know it all

Never pay back evil with more evil. Be honourable in everything you do.

Do all you can do to live at peace with everyone.

Never take revenge. Leave that to the righteous anger of God.

If your enemies are hungry feed them.

If they are thirsty give them something to drink.

Don't let evil conquer you but conquer evil by doing good."

James, the brother of Jesus, strongly connects faith and service. He affirms that our faith assures us that we are children of God and that we have been saved by His grace. Then he declares that our works are the way we make known our salvation to the world. James' most well-known and famous statement is: *"Faith without works is dead".* (James 2:26).

He is not saying that our faith is not enough to save us, but that without our faith being revealed to the world through Christ-like service, people will not be convinced of the advantage of having faith.

Like Paul, James encourages us to confront the attitudes and actions that foster unloving behaviour. He says, *"So get rid of all the filth and evil in your lives and humbly* accept *the word God has planted in your hearts, for it has the power to save your souls."* (James 1:21). Then again, like Paul, he tells the Christians he is writing to, *to serve God and people by guarding what they say, giving gifts to the poor, honouring people whatever their station in life and refraining from judging others.*

Peter writes to new Christians and in 1 Peter 5 speaking to leaders and congregations about servanthood. To elders who lead the congregations he says, *"Care for the flock that God has entrusted to you. Watch over it willingly, not grudgingly- not for what you will get out of it, but because you are eager to serve God. Don't lord it over the people assigned to your care but lead them by your own good example. And when the Great Shepherd appears you will receive a crown of never-ending glory and honor."*

(NLT)

For Further Study

Read Romans 12:9-21 again. Study and comment on the following statements:

"Don't Just pretend to love others. Really love them." (v9)

Love each other with genuine affection and take delight in honouring each other.(10) Be patient in trouble and keep on praying. (v12)

When God's people are in need, be ready to help them. (v13)

Never pay back evil with more evil. (v17)

Chapter Ten

The Apostle Paul's Instructions to Timothy

CHAPTER TEN

THE APOSTLE PAUL'S INSTRUCTIONS TO TIMOTHY

Christian leaders today are often well aware of what Paul taught Timothy about the roles and behaviours of elders, deacons and the members of the congregations in the Churches he planted in Ephesus. These instructions were meant to be part of his responsibility as a teacher. However, we may not be as familiar with Paul's instructions to Timothy about *what he* as a leader should see as imperatives for servant leadership.

> *"Timothy, my son, here are my instructions for you based on the prophetic words spoken about you earlier. May they help you fight well in the Lord's battles. Cling to your faith in Christ and keep your conscience clear. For some have deliberately violated their consciences; as a result, their faith has been shipwrecked."*
>
> 1 Timothy 1:18-19. (NLT).

Cling to your faith in Christ. This is the first and most important of Paul's instructions and to press his point he uses the examples of Hymenaeus and Alexander, two teachers who had been seduced by Satan to believe and teach false doctrine in relation to the resurrection. They gradually lost sight of their earlier belief that faith in the risen Christ was central to their ministry to others.

It is by faith that we believe God has called us to serve Him and others. It is by faith that we believe that God will provide us with the wisdom and grace to serve well. It is by faith that we seek to imitate Christ. It makes sense that Paul would encourage Timothy to cling to his faith.

"Pray for all people. Ask God to help them; intercede on their behalf and give thanks for them."

1 Timothy 2:1

Pray! Petition! Intercede! Thank! These are clear instructions as to the servant leader's priorities. Before we teach and preach, pray. Before we counsel or rebuke others, petition God on behalf of those who stumble or are in error. Stand daily before God and intercede on behalf of those who need God's help and deliverance. And always thank God for those you lead and to whom you minister and for those who minister to others.

Imagine the impact on yourself and others if, before every leaders' meeting, or while preparing Sunday's sermon, or prior to every pastoral counselling session, you engaged in prayer, petition, intercession and thanksgiving. Paul stresses the importance of this instruction by saying, *"This is good and pleases God our Saviour, who wants everyone to be saved and to understand the truth."* (1 Timothy 2:3).

During our time when serving in a growing church in a Melbourne suburb, I (Graeme) made it a priority to meet with the chairperson of the board during the week leading up to our next meeting. We would pray over the agenda and intercede on behalf of each of the staff and the elders.

Like all churches we faced challenges and difficult decisions, but we experienced a beautiful commitment to the importance of unity. We learnt that unity did not need conformity — it needed embracing and practising this instruction.

Pray! Petition! Intercede! Give thanks!

Paul now tells the young Timothy that while physical training is good, training for godliness is much better because it produces "*benefits in this life and in the life to come.*" (1 Timothy 4:8).

Elsewhere in Scripture we are told to pursue godliness. Have we always done that? Sadly no! Sometimes we have pursued agendas that have more to do with our needs and passions than they have to do with godliness. The next instruction Timothy receives is powerful.

> *"Be an example to all believers in what you say, in the way you live, in your love, your faith, and your purity ... focus on reading the scriptures to the church, encouraging the believers and teaching them."* (1 Timothy 4:12-13).

Obedience to this instruction is the key aspect of servant leadership.

Be an example! Encourage! Teach! Don't just tell people what they should say, and how they should live and love. Model it! We may be activists, goal setters, change makers, team leaders, youth pastors, theologians, pastors or teachers; but if the central focus of our ministry is not being an example, we have no power or right to do what God has called us to do. The truth is ... the most powerful, most well connected, most loving being of all time, Jesus Christ was — for His obedience — made to be Head of the Church, His body. And as Head of the Church, He not only calls us to imitate Him, but to encourage and teach those we pastor and lead.

Have the great servant leaders we have known always been perfect examples? No! Have the great servant leaders of history, except Christ, always been perfect servant leaders? No! They were effective servant leaders because being an example was their focus. When what they said or how they lived, or loved, fell short of Christlikeness, they were ready to repent and be restored. Their humility and submission to Christ, in times of weakness, was as much an example to those they led or ministered to, as what they said and how they lived and loved.

The very next instruction that Timothy received touches on something that is often ignored or treated as controversial. *"Do not neglect the spiritual gift you received through the prophecy spoken over you when the elders of the Church laid their hands on you."* (1 Timothy 4:14).

'Do not neglect the spiritual gift you have received'! When Paul wrote to the church at Ephesus, he told them that they were all recipients of a spiritual gift or gifts given by God, through the Holy Spirit, to equip them to fulfil their role as part of the Body of Christ. Now he tells Timothy, *'Don't neglect the gift you received when the elders ordained and commissioned you!'* As followers of Christ, we may be empowered at specific times and on specific occasions by the Holy Spirit, to function in ways

that transcend our knowledge or our natural abilities, and that is a wonderful reminder that we can always trust God to work in us and through us. However, even more importantly, is the truth that we each have a special gift or gifts from God that Paul said we should not neglect.

We are not told what gifts Timothy was given but we might reasonably assume, from the context of this instruction that it may have been that of pastor/teacher. However, the truth is, that as part of Christ's body, the church, each of us have received gifts. You may be a schoolteacher, university professor, a nurse, a doctor, a tradesperson, a business executive, a secretary, a full-time parent, a student or a farmer, but embedded amongst all of your acquired skills and knowledge and life experience, is a special gift or gifts given to you by the Holy Spirit.

When Paul instructed Timothy not to neglect his gift, he was instructing him both to acknowledge it and practise it. Not neglecting our gift also includes finding, as Paul did, young believers, like Timothy and Titus by mentoring them as they learn to live, and minister in the power of that gift.

For Further Study

In this chapter we have been looking at specific instructions that the Apostle Paul gives to young Timothy. Review each of them and come to a conclusion about what it would mean for you to adopt them as guidelines for your own life.

"Cling to your faith in Christ and keep your conscience clear." (1 Timothy 1:19). Hold tightly to your belief in who Jesus is. Son of God! Personal Saviour! Head of the Church — His Body! Great High Priest! Soon coming King!

Keep your conscience clear. (1:19) There are two ways to keep our conscience clear. (1) Never do anything wrong. (2) When you do something wrong confess it to the person you have wronged and to God. It is unlikely any of us will succeed at the first, but we all have a choice to obey the second.

Pray for all people. (2:1-3). Pray! Petition! Intercede! This is good and pleases God our Saviour.

Be an example by the way you live, in your love, your faith and your purity. Encourage Teach. (4:12-13). Do not neglect your spiritual gift. (4:14)

Chapter Eleven

The Image of a Shepherd

CHAPTER ELEVEN

THE IMAGE OF A SHEPHERD

In chapter 21 of John's gospel, he records a conversation between Jesus and Peter. Three times Jesus asks Peter, *"Do you love me?"* and three times Peter replies in the affirmative. After the first time, Jesus tells Peter, *"Then feed my lambs"* and after the second and third times he says, *"Feed my sheep"*. The inference is very clear. Peter is not being demoted for his failure but instead he is being recommissioned to the important ministry of shepherding.

Jesus, who had earlier described himself as the "Good Shepherd", who would lay down his life for the sheep, now tells Peter — and every pastor, bishop, and leader who would follow — that they were to be shepherds: caring for their flock and willing, if called to do so, to pay the supreme sacrifice.

The concept of being a shepherd suggests that, as leaders, we are called — in the words of Psalm 23 — to emulate the goals and intentions of our Good Shepherd, who leads, renews, guides, walks with us, protects, comforts, feeds, honours, and loves.

As God leads us in 'green pastures' and by 'still waters,' as pastors and leaders, we are called to take the people we shepherd to places that refresh and renew them. As preachers and teachers, we must not only challenge people but encourage them to embrace the richness and beauty of intimacy with God.

The Good Shepherd does not manipulate or dominate us, He guides us. The writer James promised that God would give us wisdom if we ask Him for it, and one of the purposes of that wisdom is to give guidance to those who need it.

The most impactful action a leader or pastor can take, is to walk with those who are passing through their darkest valleys. It is not always the valley of death — although our caring presence and availability at those times is extremely important. It may be a teenager struggling with depression. Or a parent, saddened and confused by the behaviour of their adolescent children. Or a businessperson facing bankruptcy. Or an elderly person whose pet has died. Being a shepherd requires us to walk with them.

We walked through a dark valley in 1969. Between January and July that year, Julia had three strokes and the situation we found ourselves in and the uncertain future we faced was very scary. We were in our late twenties, with four young children and my work required that I travelled far and wide and was often absent from home. The CEO of the Mission I worked for stepped up immediately, giving me all the time off that we would need on full pay. I know it meant increased workloads for him and others, but his intention was clear. Here was a leader who was prepared to walk with us through our 'darkest valley'. It made a huge impression on us. We never forgot the importance of 'walking' through valleys with those we were called to shepherd.

Our Good Shepherd has a staff to drive off our enemies and a rod to guide us back when we wander too far from Him. As 'under shepherds' we are called to always protect and sometimes correct those we lead and pastor. We must get that order right. Protection should be constant, and correction should occur only when it is needed and even then, it must be gentle, designed to build up, not to tear down.

When Jesus was preparing his disciples for their lives as Apostles, he was very aware that the life and work he was calling them too would be exacting, and their willingness to love and serve him would make them very vulnerable. Throughout each of their lives their greatest source of personal courage came from Jesus' promise, *"Be assured that I am with you, even to the end of the age."*

(Matthew 28:20).

Comforting, feeding, honouring and loving are the obvious responsibilities of pastors and leaders. These can only consistently occur when we commit ourselves to the truth of Philippians 2:36a. *"Don't be selfish, don't try to impress others. Be humble. Think of others as better than yourselves. Don't look out for your own interests but take an interest in others too. You must have the same attitude that Christ Jesus had."* Paul then goes on to speak about the humility of Jesus through strengthening others.

One of the great teachings of Jesus on leadership came, when he told Peter he would deny that he was one of Jesus' disciples. *"Satan has asked to sift each of you like wheat. But I have pleaded in prayer for you, Simon, that your faith should not fail. So, when you have repented and turned to me again, strengthen your brothers."*

(Luke 22:31).

As leaders in the Body of Christ we will not be sinless or faultless, and there will be times when we, like Peter, will need to repent and be restored to our former relationship with Christ. When we do, in true humility and vulnerability, we must speak out of our failure and restoration into the lives of those we lead and serve. What we say must be motivated by desire to strengthen others for their journey.

Listen to Peter strengthening his brothers and sisters in Christ. *"By His divine Power God has given us everything we need to live a godly life ... Because of this make every effort to respond to God's promises so add to your faith moral excellence, and to moral excellence, knowledge and to knowledge, self-control, and to self-control patient endurance, and to patient endurance, godliness, and to godliness, brotherly affection and to brotherly affection love.* (2 Peter 1: 5-7).

Do you see the important elements of this story?

Insight. Jesus had seen the enormous potential in Peter from the time of their first meeting and knew that Satan would want to bring him down.

Warning. Jesus warned Peter that Satan would sift them like wheat and that Peter would fall.

Teaching. He taught Peter that although he would be disappointed and ashamed of what he had done, his true repentance was a sure way back.

Renewal and recommission. Jesus assures Peter that when he does repent and turn back to God there is a new opportunity for ministry. A ministry that strengthens others.

But the important elements of this story do not stop there. The forgiven and restored Peter, now a recognised and respected leader of the early church, teaches that the primary goal of those who lead the people of God is not the pursuit of status or authority, but Christlikeness.

This means embracing moral excellence, growing in true knowledge of a personal relationship with Jesus, exercising self-control in leadership, and practising patient endurance when the journey becomes difficult. Being godly in their attitudes to each other, caring for each other like brothers and sisters should. And finally, to be as deeply loving to all people as Christ himself was to them. What a wonderful treasure chest of leadership tasks and priorities we have found here.

It is helpful for us to be reminded of the truth that most of the great biblical stories illustrating moral excellence, self-control, patience and godliness occur in the context of fierce opposition.

In the Old Testament, we have **David,** opposed by the Philistines, when he was just a boy armed with a sling.

Joseph was sold by his own brothers into a hostile Egypt, plotted against by his boss's wife, jailed for something he did not do. Eventually recognised and honoured for his moral excellence, divinely imparted knowledge and kindness.

Daniel's friends, all Israelites, who had risen to positions of leadership in Babylon, were thrown into a fiery furnace because their faith, knowledge of God and moral excellence would not permit them to worship the golden image of a heathen king.

Daniel himself, thrown into a lion's den because he would not obey the King's edict that praying to his God was against the royal law.

In the New Testament, **John the Baptist** was imprisoned and later beheaded for preaching that the Messiah had come. **Jesus** himself was pursued, persecuted and ultimately crucified. **Stephen was stoned. Paul** the Apostle was imprisoned, persecuted and executed because of his refusal to not stop preaching the Gospel.

Tradition says **Peter** was crucified upside down. **John** was banished to the isle of Patmos, and countless others from that time on have paid the ultimate price for their faith, moral excellence, patient endurance and love for those whom Jesus came to save.

As leaders, we need to understand that we are engaged in training … preparing people to live for and serve Christ in an oppositional, even hostile environment. Whether it be in the workplace, at school or university or even sometimes within one's own family.

We believe that among the most important decisions we have ever made was to always have a personal mentor. The importance of having a mentor was that when we set goals for ourselves, we had someone whom we knew would hold us accountable for pursuing the strategies that would enable us to reach those goals. Strategies, accountability, encouragement and coaching are invaluable elements in enhancing our physical, emotional, relational and spiritual growth.

As we encourage emerging leaders to embrace mentoring, it is vitally important that we — as current leaders — model this by having our own personal mentor. In this way, we can better encourage those who lead to also have a mentor, as well as making ourselves available to mentor others.

For Further Study

The key passages of scripture in this chapter are Psalm 23; Luke 22:31-32; John 21:15-17; 2 Peter 1:5-7. Read and meditate on these passages and seek out what God is saying about leaders being Shepherds.

There are some important functions of Shepherds. What is it about your leadership style that reflects the qualities of our Good Shepherd?

Which of these functions of leadership are evident in your own ministry and which requires some attention?

Do you lead by example?

Do you walk with others in their dark valleys? Do you comfort those who are hurt and sad?

Do you honour and respect those to whom you minister?

Chapter Twelve

Hierarchical Leadership Structures

CHAPTER TWELVE

HIERARCHICAL LEADERSHIP STRUCTURES

Many modern-day churches have hierarchical structures, like corporate organizations, with clear chains of command and authority. We understand the reason for this. We live in complex times. We have also seen the catastrophic and sometimes tragic consequences of unaccountable leadership. These consequences convince us of the need for constitutions, legislated child protection laws, fair work laws to protect staff, rules for ethical conduct and financial accountability.

On one hand, the Bible declares that the universal Church, Christ's body, is not subject to any authority other than Christ himself. Consider what Paul writes in Ephesians 1:19-23.

> *"I also pray that you will understand the incredible greatness of God's power for us who believe Him. This is the same mighty power that raised Christ from the dead and seated Him in the place of honour at Gods right hand in the heavenly realms. Now he is far above any ruler or authority or power or leader or anything else- not only in this world but also in the world to come. God has put all things under the authority of Christ and has made Him head over all things for the benefit of the Church. And the Church is His body; it is made full and complete by Christ, who fills all things with himself."*

When it comes to ethical and behavioural issues in both the universal Church and the local congregation, our ultimate and perfect example is Christ Jesus himself, and our accountability for how we treat others is also to him. If in our local churches we constantly affirmed Jesus as our living head and modelled our lives and behaviours on him ... then our children would be safe ... our professional pastoral and administrative staff would be treated fairly ... and our conduct when providing food and activities would be of the highest standards. As bona fide communities within our cities or towns, we would be seen as examples of excellence.

On the other hand, when a church leader is appointed to the role of lead pastor or chairperson of the board, the assumption is that — whatever administrative structure they develop or inherit, and whatever leadership style they adopt — one of their key roles is to oversee adherence to the regulations and requirements which are legislated by their denomination or the state.

Whilst we agree with the importance of this, as pastors we must also be aware of the subtle ways it can divert our commitment to serving our living God and one another with Christlike hearts. Such diversion occurs when administrative demands begin to take priority over the primary tasks Jesus has commanded us to fulfil i.e. living, teaching, counselling, worshipping, serving, pastoring, evangelizing and discipling.

The success of a leader or leadership team is often measured by efficiency and the achievement of measurable outcomes such as congregational growth, facility development and maintenance, and financial stability.

These measures shape the leadership style adopted by pastors and board members, with charismatic or transformational models favoured for their emphasis on vision, motivation, and personal influence. They also increase the administrative burden in both human resources and financial cost.

Conversely, in local churches where the measurable goals relate to evangelism and producing loving, serving disciples who show practical care for each other and the wider community, something additional to the chosen model of leadership is required. The pastors and board members must work toward a servanthood model of church life that emphasises teaching, modelling, and empowering the congregation to participate in setting, pursuing, assessing, and achieving the goals to which they are committed.

The question of whether the radical, servant-hearted leadership model Jesus demonstrated and taught can survive and flourish is a profound one. It becomes especially complex when the church feels obligated to operate under denominational rules and the regulations imposed by secular governments.

The issue that must be addressed is that Jesus' leadership model is characterized by humility, self-sacrifice, and a focus on serving others rather than seeking authority and control. This model contrasts sharply with many secular leadership models adopted by the Church which prioritize authority, charisma, individualism and organizational efficiency.

While the local church must adhere to certain regulations and requirements, it is crucial that the believers maintain the core values of servanthood and community. This involves creating a culture where serving others is valued and practiced by everyone, from the leaders to the congregational members. The emphasis in creating such a culture should be on humility, empathy, and selflessness, promoting a servant mindset within the community.

On one occasion we arrived at the church we regularly attend an hour before the first of the two morning services were scheduled to commence. We were amazed at the hive of joyful activity we had walked into. The musicians and singers were busy practising ... the Kids' Church team were setting up ... the welcomers and car park attendants had just finished their prayer and briefing time ... and the coffee team was already preparing for the rest of the congregation to arrive. We were very impressed. In Jesus' model of leadership these servants 'were the greatest among us'.

In this particular local church, the leaders have created a multitude of opportunities for people to serve: a food pantry for the wider community, several playgroups, a Boys' Brigade, fifty life groups, and an emergency meals service — each primarily led and staffed by volunteers. These ministries are underpinned by a deliberate integration of servanthood principles into all teaching and training, and the mission statement reflects a clear intention to equip people to "be Christ in every place."

Fostering a culture of servanthood within a community or organization involves creating an environment where serving others is valued and practiced by everyone. Here are some key strategies to expand on this concept:

Lead by example:

In churches that are committed to creating a caring and serving community, leaders play a crucial role in setting the tone for servanthood. When the leaders demonstrate a willingness to serve, it sets a powerful example for others to follow. This can be done through everyday actions, such as helping with tasks that are not part of their job description, showing genuine concern for others' well-being, and being approachable and supportive.

It is clear from Paul's instructions to Titus — a church planter on the island of Crete, that the example a pastor/leader sets, either validates or contradicts his or her teaching. *"And you yourself must be an example to them by doing good works of every kind. Let everything you do reflect the integrity and seriousness of your teaching. Teach the truth so that your teaching cannot be criticized. Then those who oppose us will be ashamed and have nothing bad to say about us."* (Titus 2: 7-8).

Create opportunities for service:

Leaders of churches who build and maintain a servanthood culture regularly organize and promote opportunities for all their members to engage in acts of community service. This can include volunteering at local shelters, participating in local community projects, or organizing charity events. By providing structured opportunities for service, they make it easier for people to get involved and experience the joy of serving others.

Incorporate servanthood into teaching:

Pastors of servanthood-focused churches integrate the principles of humility and servanthood into sermons, bible studies, and educational programs. They use examples from the Bible, such as Jesus washing the disciples' feet, to illustrate the importance of serving others, encouraging discussions on how these principles can be applied in everyday life.

There are many pastors who are zealous about teaching sound doctrine and defending the truth. They preach the gospel and invite people to receive Christ. They baptize new believers and organise courses on discipleship. Despite all this, the words of Jesus to the Church in Ephesus might well apply to their church:

> *"I know all the things you do. I have seen your hard work and your patient endurance. I know you don't tolerate evil people. You have examined the claims of those who say they are apostles but are not. You have discovered they are liars. You have patiently suffered for me without quitting. But I have this complaint against you. You don't love me or each other as you did at first. Look how far you have fallen. Turn back to me and do the works you did at first. If you don't repent, I will come and remove your lampstand from its place among the churches. But you have this in your favour. You hate the evil deeds of the Nicolaitans as I do."*
>
> (Revelation 2: 2-6).

Jesus commended them for their hard work, originally based on their love for him and each other. But now is driven by their disapproval of the Nicolaitans as well as a commitment to stand against the sect's false doctrine by unswervingly pursuing sound doctrine. However, in doing so, their love for Jesus and each other had waned. This is so important to Jesus that he calls them to repent and turn back to where they were at first.

Recognize and acknowledge all acts of service:

Pastors and leaders of servanthood focused churches maintain a culture of servanthood by acknowledging acts of servanthood within the church community. Leaders can achieve this by simply meeting regularly with the various ministry teams. Such recognition of service not only encourages those who serve but also inspires others to follow their example.

Some people will argue that our reward comes from God, for whom the service was performed, and will quote Scriptures such as Matthew 6:4 and Hebrews 6:10. This is true of course, but because individual acts of service are done by a person who belongs to the Body of Christ, it is appropriate for the other parts of the body to value those acts of service. Churches with a servanthood culture promote values such as humility, empathy, and selflessness within the community. They encourage individuals to consider how they can serve others in their daily lives, whether it's through small acts of kindness or more regular commitments to a team or organisation. These churches always foster an environment where people feel valued and appreciated for their contributions.

Provide training and resources:

Churches that seek to encourage their members to serve one another and the wider community offer workshops and training sessions that equip individuals with the skills and knowledge needed to serve effectively. This can include practical skills — such as cooking for large groups, basic carpentry, or first aid — as well as training for service in specific contexts, including hospitality, caregiving, and pastoral care. Importantly, such training should always include ways for people to recognise the giftings they have. It is when people are using the gifts of the Spirit in their lives that they are most productive and fulfilled.

Foster a supportive community:

Leaders of servanthood-focused churches aim to create a supportive and loving environment where everyone feels valued and empowered. They encourage open communication, mutual respect, and cooperation. When people feel supported and appreciated by the leadership, they are more likely to engage in acts of service that contribute to the community.

Encourage personal reflection and growth:

Leaders in servanthood-focused churches encourage individuals to reflect on their own experiences of servanthood and consider how they can grow in this area. This can be done through journalling, prayer, and meditation focused on servanthood. They provide opportunities for people to share their reflections and experiences with others, fostering a sense of shared growth and learning. The whole point of utilizing any or all of these strategies is to build a culture of servanthood that imitates the love, humility and sacrificial leadership of Jesus Christ.

For Further Study

Ephesians 1:19-23 speaks about the headship of Christ over the Church, his body. Many of the functions of a local church, are subject to regulations established by the State, as is also the case for secular bodies. However, when it comes to the essential ministry of the Church, it is Christ's authority, commissioning and empowerment, that distinguishes the Church from a secular organisation.

How is this truth reflected in your ministry?

In Titus 2:7-8 Paul instructs Titus on leadership. Examine some of the areas of your own ministry in the light of these verses.

In Revelation 2:1-7 Jesus commends the Church for some of the things that they do but rebukes them for not loving Him and each other as they once did. He calls them to repentance. As you look at your church now, and then as it once was, what might Jesus call it to repent of?

Chapter Thirteen

Changed Lives ... Empowered Leadership

CHAPTER THIRTEEN

CHANGED LIVES ... EMPOWERED LEADERSHIP

Before we attempt to change the culture of the congregation we serve or the team we lead, let's examine some of the changes that may need to occur in us as leaders.

- What are the challenges we face when it comes to humility, forgiveness, love, kindness, gentleness and generosity?
- Are we good at dealing with conflict?
- Are we patient in handling difficult or fractious people?
- Do we get angry too quickly?
- Do we become anxious when we cannot control each of the circumstances and situations that arise?
- Do we look too often for the affirmation of others and react to negative comments and criticisms?

All these attitudes and behaviours and many others will always work against us being good examples of servanthood-leadership. If your answer to one or more of the questions above, is yes, please seek help from someone to enable you to understand why it is so and how you might begin to change this behaviour.

We need to speak for a moment here about the

helpfulness of seeking counselling. It is universally acknowledged that the behaviours listed above are often closely related to unresolved pain in our lives. Traumatic events such as physical, sexual, emotional, or verbal abuse, as well as childhood bullying, frequently leave survivors with unresolved and painful emotions. These wounds often lie at the root of lifelong anxiety, shame, and anger. Other negative life events, although not traumatic, may have similar long-term impacts on our adult behaviour.

What are these negative behaviours that need to be owned and changed? Chronic control, a lack of patience with people, a tendency to withdraw from others, an inability to listen deeply, and many other angry and dismissive reactions.

As mentioned earlier, for several years we had the privilege of organizing and leading Ministry Enrichment programs at Elkanah, in Marysville. Pastors from all over Australia and New Zealand, along with their husband or wife attended these three-week residential retreats. Early in the retreat each participant would complete two different personality profiles: The Taylor-Johnson Temperament Analysis and the Edwards Personal Preference Schedule. Following the assessment of the results they had the opportunity to meet with a counsellor and have follow-up sessions if they chose.

While the tests were often viewed skeptically by many at the beginning of the course, they revealed so much about the way they functioned that they often jokingly asked if they could take them home and run their whole congregation through them. The insights they gained were remarkable, and from the feedback we have received over the years, we know that the counselling was often transformative in the way they understood and practised ministry.

An Example of a Helpful Counselling Model

The counselling approach we found most helpful was based on Rational Emotive Behaviour Therapy (REBT) which was first developed by psychologist Albert Ellis in the 1950's, and was later adapted by a well-known Christian psychotherapist, Dr. Larry Crabb, as an effective Christian counselling model.

This approach is based on the idea that most of our emotional and behavioural difficulties do not stem from the events themselves, but from the irrational beliefs and interpretations we hold about those events. When we identify and confront these irrational beliefs, and replace them with more constructive thinking patterns, it leads to improved emotional well-being, increased resilience, and healthier and more adaptive behaviours.

It looks somewhat like this:

Painful events ➜ *Irrational Beliefs*

Irrational Beliefs ➜ *Painful Emotions*

Painful Emotions ➜ *Damaging behaviours*

Painful Event:

A painful event occurs when something happens that changes your environment, threatens your physical or mental health, destroys a relationship and diminishes your sense of self-worth. The event may be the result of choices someone else has made or it may be the result of your own choice. It may also have been an accident or medical emergency that was beyond yours or any other person's control. On the other hand it might just be growing up without the normal affirmations and feelings of acceptance.

Irrational or Untrue Beliefs:

In response to one or more events, you developed — and may still hold — beliefs about yourself and others that are irrational and untrue. These beliefs have negatively shaped your self-concept, your view of life, and your perception of others. They are also a primary source of the painful emotions you experience.

Painful Emotions:

As a result of the beliefs you hold about yourself and others, you struggle with painful emotions such as anger, bitterness, shame, guilt, resentment, anxiety, or depression. These emotions are shaped by irrational or untrue beliefs, not by the events themselves.

Damaging Behaviours:

Common damaging behaviours that may affect those close to us are cynicism, criticism, sarcasm, social withdrawal, and a quick temper. Internalised painful emotions can result in unhealthy dependencies, addictions, mental illness and acts of violence.

The stark truth is that 'hurt' people ... hurt people!

Our behaviours and the responses of loved ones that are hurt by them serve to confirm our negative beliefs and so the cycle continues not only in our lifetime but from generation to generation. That it is why making a resolve to heal and pursuing appropriate help to do so is important.

In his book, *Effective Christian Counselling*, Dr. Larry Crabb presents an approach to counselling based on the psychological principles of Rational Emotive Behaviour Therapy. He applies these principles within the context of the Bible as a reliable authority for understanding people, diagnosing problems, and prescribing solutions. The scriptures provide the framework for both the goals and the methods of counselling. We ourselves have come to realise that even experienced, spirit-filled leaders need to avail themselves of the type of one-to-one counselling that causes them to ask searching questions.

Some questions most of us need to ask not once ... but often, are:

- Do I really believe that Jesus' grace of forgiveness is not only for me but for those who have hurt me?
- Is there anyone in my past or recent life that I have not forgiven?
- Do I recognise a damaging behaviour that may have its origins in my unforgiveness of myself or someone else? Am I over controlling, critical, cynical or quick to get angry?
- Do I suffer from depression or anxiety?

There have been times when the ancient proverb 'Physician heal thyself', has powerfully applied to us and to many a faithful pastor. The factor that we cannot escape is that we are not often able to heal ourselves without the skillful and compassionate help of another. We might shrink back from this reality, but it is in setting aside all our concerns and preconceived ideas and seeking the help of a counsellor who shares our values and beliefs, that hope lies.

As we have already stated several times, the Bible teaches that humans are created in the image of God and are designed for relationship with God and others.

Our deepest needs for significance and security are ultimately met in God, not in self-effort or worldly achievements. The Bible recognizes the reality of sin — humanity's choice to live independent of God — and the resulting brokenness in human relationships and inner life. True healing and growth come through reconciliation with God and transformation by the Holy Spirit.

The local church is God's primary instrument for healing, growth, and support. Ministering to broken people is not just for professionals, although serious therapy is the responsibility of those who have the appropriate training. The truth remains that all caring Christians within the church community, are called to *"bear one another's burdens"* (Galatians 6:2).

The goal of counselling is not just symptom relief, but spiritual maturity — helping people become more like Christ in character and relationships. This involves repentance, faith, obedience, and growing in love for God and others. Biblical truth challenges and replaces wrong beliefs, encourages confession and forgiveness, and fosters dependence on God's grace. The process of healing, change and growth is relational, rooted in love and humility.

The life and work of a servant leader consists of leading well and empowering others to serve according to their spiritual giftedness. But it also involves the care of our own hearts and minds. Fears and doubts — rather than being internalised — can and should be addressed. Anger and resentment which damage our relationships with God and others, must be confessed and repented of. Wounds and hurts can be completely healed.

We choose to end this book with the words of the Apostle Peter:

> *"By His divine power God has given us everything we need for living a godly life. We have received all of this by coming to know him, the one who called us to Himself by means of His marvelous glory and excellence. And because of His glory and excellence, He has given us great and precious promises. These are the promises that enable you to share His divine nature and escape the world's corruption caused by human desires. In view of all this, make every effort to respond to God's promises. Supplement your faith with a generous provision of moral excellence, and moral excellence with knowledge, and knowledge with self-control, and self-control with patient endurance, and patient endurance with godliness, and godliness with brotherly affection, and brotherly affection with love for everyone. The more you grow like this, the more productive and useful you*

will be in your knowledge of our Lord Jesus Christ. But those who fail to develop in this way are short-sighted or blind, forgetting that they have been cleansed from their old sins.

So, dear brothers and sisters, work hard to prove that you really are among those God has called and chosen. Do these things, and you will never fall away. Then God will give you a grand entrance into the eternal Kingdom of our Lord and Saviour Jesus Christ." (2 Peter 1:3-11).

For Further Study

Read 2 Peter 1:3-9 again. Study it more deeply by dividing it into five statements.

1. Verse 3.

"By His divine power God has given us everything we need for a godly life. We have received all this by coming to know Him. The One who has called us to himself by means of His marvelous glory and excellence."

2. Verse 4.

"Because of His glory and excellence, He has given us great and precious promises. These are the promises that enable you to share His divine nature and escape the worlds corruption caused by human desires."

3. Verse 5-7. *"In view of all this make every effort to respond to Gods promises. Supplement your faith with a generous provision of moral excellence and moral excellence with knowledge, and knowledge with self-control, and self-control with patient endurance, and patient endurance with godliness, and godliness with brotherly affection and brotherly affection with love for everyone."*

4. Verse 8–9 *"The more you grow like this, the more useful and productive you will be in your knowledge of our Lord Jesus Christ. But those who fail to develop in this way are shot-sighted or blind, forgetting that they have been cleansed from their old sins."*

5. Verse 10–11. *"So dear brothers and sisters work hard to prove that you are really among those God has called and chosen. Do these things and you will never fall away. Then God will give you a grand entrance into the eternal Kingdom of our Lord and Saviour Jesus Christ"*

ABOUT THE AUTHORS

Graeme Cann is the author of six books and has co-authored three other books with his wife Julia. They have been married for sixty-three years and have four children, fourteen grandchildren and seven great-grandchildren. During their marriage, they spent ten years with the Leprosy Mission, four years as youth pastors, sixteen years leading the Elkanah Community at Marysville and twenty-eight years pastoring Churches. Since retiring in 2017, they continue to share their life experiences further ... through writing and mentoring pastors. They live in Pakenham, Victoria, Australia.

For further information visit their website:
www.graemecann.com

www.ingramcontent.com/pod-product-compliance
Lightning Source LLC
Chambersburg PA
CBHW042116100526
44587CB00025B/4073